HEART OF THE CARDS

A Fool's Journey

Andrew Greig

HEART OF THE CARDS
© 2024 **Andrew Greig**

ISBN: 978-1-7385255-0-8 Paperback

Published by Inspired By Publishing

Cover Design: Tanya Grant

The strategies in this book are presented primarily for enjoyment and educational purposes. Every effort has been made to trace copyright holders and obtain their permission for the use of copyright material.

The information and resources provided in this book are based upon the author's personal experience. Any outcome, income statements or other results, are based on the author's experience and there is no guarantee that your experience will be the same. There is an inherent risk in any business enterprise or activity and there is no guarantee that you will have similar results as the author as a result of reading this book.

The author reserves the right to make changes and assumes no responsibility or liability whatsoever on behalf of any purchaser or reader of these materials.

Acknowledgements

The most important message goes to my two daughters, you both are the inspiration in my life and without you, I would have no life. My reason for pushing my own boundaries and reaching higher heights stems from a desire to show you exactly what could be achieved by determination, hard work, and an unwavering belief in what you are doing. I hope you both always remember to maintain a wonder in life and an attitude of fun. Your limitations are not determined by anyone else. Live your life how you want while taking lessons and inspirations from all around you.

I must express gratitude to anyone who has ever touched my life, too many to name but for both the good and bad, without your influence on my life, I would not be who I am and certainly would not be in the position to write this project of passion.

To the mad few who have stuck by me despite everything, thanks for giving me faith in humanity and for the happy memories I can bring forward any time I feel down.

I would like to say how I am especially grateful to my Mum, Stepdad, Auntie and Uncle (Mum's side). You have all given me so much more than you realize.

Special thanks to Annie Rees photography for the image used on the back cover and for the amazing work during and after the shoot.

Finally, I would like to thank you as well, dear reader. For being interested enough to pick this up and dedicate some of your precious time to reading my story, your support is gratefully received, and I hope you take something positive from this to enhance your own life or forge your own path.

Remember, if a single person is inspired to take positive actions in their life because you made the gargantuan effort to get out of bed. Every tear shed, every ache, each hardship has been worth it. It was truly worth getting out of bed.

Contents

Introduction

Greetings reader and a great many thanks for investing your energy into this book. Before reading, it's important to maintain an open mind. I imagine you already have given that you picked this up.

My name is Andrew Greig, and I am, among other things, a Tarot reader. Now that itself carries some stigma and broad stereotypes, such as the tarot being evil and demonic, only used by gypsies, practitioners of black magic and by people who are otherwise involved with the occult. I hope to break those stereotypes during this book. This is not an in-depth look at the Tarot cards, there are many other great resources for that, and besides, I don't want to put myself out of a job. This is more along the lines of a memoir to the development of a Tarot reader and some of the stories and experiences that have shaped my journey. I want to help people understand what they don't understand and let them see that behind every Tarot reader, there is a human. Not a Satan worshiper or a witch (Some might be, but then again, so might your doctor).

It's my wish to break these stereotypes and give you a more human aspect of Tarot. Its uses and benefits for any who is trusting enough to explore it with a skilled reader.

This will follow a very basic structure because I am a very basic person. I hope it's easy for you all to follow and more importantly, enjoy the journey. I will divulge some of my own history and upbringing to give context to my development and cover a brief history of Tarot, the structure of a Tarot deck of cards with a general explanation of the cards with some stories about certain ones and how they affected my own readings. But for extra context I use my own journey so you can understand how you can relate the meanings into your own (although different) situations.

From there I will explain the basics behind a reading and the process of conducting oneself during one. I have tried to cover as much I possibly could without boring you while keeping enough back so you could find out more if you so desired.

As you might deduce from my introduction, this is a very personal project for me, and it has been something I have placed a lot of energy into. I have also changed the names of people for confidentiality reasons.

Disclaimer. I will be talking about some quite difficult topics including physical and sexual abuse. Although these are not explored in depth. I feel they are relevant to mention because were it not for these experiences, I most definitely would not be who and what I am today. I also swear on occasion, usually for dramatic emphasis or comedic timing. You have been warned.

With that being said and understood. Take that leap of faith with me and I will see you at the World.

Lots of love,
Andrew

Chapter 1:
<u>Creating the Fool</u>

Before I proceed, allow me to properly introduce myself. I was born and grew up in a fishing town called Peterhead in the Northeast of Scotland. Currently the population is around 19,000, it used to be a little less. Although there is a rich history in the whaling industry, previous incarnation as a popular resort town due to its scenery and amazing beaches, known as one of the biggest white fishing ports in Europe and a prison with a colorful history and the subject of an SAS operation. Peterhead doesn't really have much going for it from the outside, in fact people who are from Peterhead or who have moved from elsewhere usually respond to the question. "How is it in Peterhead?" The common response is, "Aye, it's a strange place."

As you would imagine it was the kind of place where you break wind in public in the morning and by late afternoon people were organizing a collection for your funeral. The most valuable commodity was and still is gossip. Everyone loved to know everything about everyone while protecting their own situation for fear of being a victim of someone else's gossip. This aspect of the town has dwindled over the years due to incomers to the town and people being generally less sociable (globally not just in Peterhead).

As you might expect, being a small community, it was quite isolated from events outside of the local area. So, as communications improved, industries changed and awareness of options and opportunities increased, people started to move out of the town for work in the City of Aberdeen and further afield, this small mind mentality also started to disappear. Of course, there are still elements of it there but it's not as bad. The opinions of others were always held in high regard, mainly for fear of a scandal developing and people being left "Black Affronted" (local speak for being extremely embarrassed). The dialect mostly spoken was Doric, so some words make no sense unless you are from this part of the country.

Exposure to other cultures and ways of life has also caused this aspect of the town to become diluted. My own accent has changed over the years as I am required to be able to communicate effectively to a broad range of people in my work.

As I grew up during the late 80's and 90's, which was, I think during, probably the fastest period of change in the world, at least in terms of exposure to new technology and societal beliefs. It's often hard to keep track of where we are now as things are so fluid nowadays. The last of the old school as it were. I was to find out as I worked in different places and met different people and became aware of different societal trends that how I was raised and what I grew up with wasn't the way things had to be done, this as you can imagine was very confusing as I got older.

Now, Peterhead as I have painted it would not normally be the type of place that would produce a Tarot reader, at least not one who would openly admit it. Church and Christianity and those traditional beliefs were a big part of the town and to this present age it maintains that ingrained attitudes towards anything even remotely different – at least in the context that I am writing. Of course, any lingering prejudice towards anything different, Peterhead has, nonetheless, had to adapt to the ever-changing world but in terms of exploring holistic therapies, spiritualism and in general the esoteric and often misunderstood aspect of Tarot. It has been slow.

Although it is my hometown, I have very little nostalgia for Peterhead, it has never really felt like home. I have always been a little (big) bit different.

More often than not, I was thought of as being homosexual because I have always been open to exploring my feminine more than my masculine energies (this balance improved as I got older). In addition to my preference for spending time with the girls in my class, it didn't help with changing the assumption. I would be teased for hanging around and talking with the girls and not playing football, it was discouraged by adults around me as well. So, as I grew up, I didn't have many friends, at times I might have been around people, but I always felt like an outsider. Peterhead wasn't an easy place for me to grow up and as I will touch on later, there were quite a lot of traumas associated with my upbringing that helped shape me into who and what I am. I was always an easy target; for one, I was a strange little fat kid.

My environment was less than ordinary for the time, I lived with a single mum. She is an amazing woman, and always does what she thinks is best. I learned a lot from her work ethic, she was always working hard to provide my younger brother and myself with what we needed. She often worked two jobs and despite how hard it must have been for her; she was always able to keep going. My father was alcohol and drug addicted, generally absent in my life (I only have a few memories of him being sober and the rest ... Well, you will need to wait for my full autobiography to find out). He was murdered when I was 17.

I also grew up in an undesirable part of the town, the sounds of intoxicated arguments and women shrieking with terror as their partner beat them were common around there. It was normal to see a woman walking around town with thick black sunglasses to hide the bruises and swelling on her face.

Don't get me wrong, it wasn't all bad, there was generally a lovely sense of community around the neighbors and the street was connected in ways very uncommon these days. People would visit, check in and on the fine days would congregate while the children would play. I used to love the game of curby. (we would stand on opposite sides of the road and try to bounce a ball off the opposing curb for points). We would roam the fields around and explore the beaches.

But, nice as some of these moments were, it's the bad things that stand out and ultimately shape a person, character building they say it is.

Because of the lack of a male figure in my early life I have always been more comfortable around women because my Auntie and Grunny (Grandmother in Doric) lived in the same street and were round often, my mums' friends visited often as well.

I used to enjoy listening to them talk and complain and gossip from a young age. This is how I learned what was proper and improper behaviors for a man to exhibit and morals to follow. So, I have always tried to be the kind of man that these women around me talked about. "You wouldn't do that would you, Andrew?" they would sometimes ask me. I always wanted to protect them and didn't want anyone to be talking about me in the way they all talked about the men in their lives. "You should be grateful if he doesn't hit you." was something of an ironic statement, it's amazing and frightening what could be accepted over time if it isn't challenged.

Because of this, my preference to be around women has always been obvious (being that most of the spiritual community is female, that hasn't changed) but it has caused quite a lot of tension over the years to the point where relationships and friendships have been affected. I'm a friendzone kind of guy and I don't even fight it anymore, but usually that ends when my friends meet someone who can't handle a male friend on the scene. If I'm at a social event I am normally around the females because I can't contribute much if the guys are speaking about football or work. I find deeper conversations tend to be with the women.

My contact with my dad (or lack of, would be more accurate) and his side of the family was quite limited. But they had an impact on me. He had two brothers and a sister. I don't have many memories of his sister outside of her bringing my cousin round to play every so often. One of his brothers, because he was also drug dependent was generally off the scene. But the other brother, now he was a c*nt.

Although I can't recall the exact age, I was young when I first experienced sexual abuse from multiple people.

Because my parents were apart from an early age, my abusers didn't have regular access to me. So the events were spread out. These events would happen when I was visiting some people or would be ushered in if I was spotted walking alone. Normally when there was nobody else to act as witness, they would remind me that they would do the same thing to my mum and younger brother if I told anyone. As I got older and bigger, the sexual abuse stopped and it turned more into humiliation and physical abuse. Often just the threat of it was enough to instill terror.

One day I was walking back to school along the liney (old train line), I was 11 and one of my abusers was walking towards me. Nobody else was around at the time so my heart instantly froze. He smiled at me with his cold monstrous gaze and charged me into a fence. I was frozen with panic as the fence wires pressed into my face. My body tightened as it prepared for a strike, but I felt something against my temple, as he turned me round to face him and held my throat with enough pressure to restrict my breathing but not tight enough to choke me into a cough. I saw that he held a gun to my head and was laughing and screaming about how easy it would be for him to kill me and nobody would give a sh*t. The cold steel and sharp point of the barrel hurt as he twisted it round before lowering it slowly under my chin.

I'm man enough to admit I did soil myself a little. His eyes were wide and full of hatred, it was like I was looking at pure evil, a demon. Then he started laughing harder, more maniacally and pulled the trigger and howled even more with glee as he informed me that I was such a "poof" for "being feart (scared) of a fake gun." He released his grip and walked away as if nothing had happened.

Panic held me static for some time before I could move my paralysed legs. I was shaking so much I didn't know how to react, who could I tell? Who would believe me? I hid behind a fence until I could stop crying because I didn't want anyone passing to see or tease me and even more so, because I still had an afternoon of school to deal with and I knew that some of the bullies would be waiting for me and if they thought I had been crying it would give them additional excuse to torment me. That was the kind of 'man' he was. I never told anyone that story before, so you have borne witness to the first telling of it.

So, I didn't have a strong male role model growing up until I was around 13 years old when my mum met my stepdad and we moved into his country house when I was around 14. Any time I refer to my old man in conversation, I'm referring to my stepdad. He has taught me a lot of what it means to be a man, even if he doesn't realize it himself. I will always be grateful to him for putting up with what he did, my brother and I couldn't have been an easy take on. Among the best advices I have ever received came from him. When I was 17, I was in a bad place, and it got worse over time. "You die if you worry, and you die if you don't. So why worry?" he said to me. I didn't take much notice of it at the time as you tend to block everything else out when you're lost in darkness. But I often think of those words.

As protecting others was a big part of my core belief I wouldn't retaliate when bullied because I didn't want to cause any hurt to them or make their parents worried and to prevent my mum any extra stresses, I hid how bad it actually was. Certainly, when I got older and started to deal with other more traumatic experiences many of what I had inflicted upon me was hidden from the world until I decided to forgive and speak about it.

A big part of my childhood was surrounded in fear because of what I experienced. My mum and other adults used to tell me that school was the best years of my life, "F**k if it's going to get worse, I want out now." I would think. I absolutely HATED (I don't like that word, buts it's true) school. My primary school years from four (I started at four instead of five because I was basically a genius), until 11 was filled with being generally picked on by classmates and some of the teachers. I remember in early primary school my teacher would sometimes hit me (not hard enough to bruise) and lock me in dark cupboards, she did punish the other bairns (kids) as well, but she seemed to really have a special hatred for me as they didn't get the same jib as me.

Other children would notice this, and I would get blamed for many things. There was one boy who really took to winding me up. He came up to me once in class during an art session, cut my trouser pocket and then his own. He ran up and told the teacher I had done it to him, even though he still held the scissors and I had clearly been drawing and painting. She hauled me from my chair and threw me into the cupboard once again. My mum was the only one who believed me.

I was always easily distracted and generally uninterested in school and most of the little concerns of the other bairns. I was lost in my thoughts much of the time and daydreaming about being a hero and saving the world by getting rid of all the bad people. I am certain that nowadays I would be diagnosed with something.

When I was eight and on the 1ˢᵗ day of the summer holidays, I was hit by a car and injured quite badly. I was in a coma for a few days, and I think it was touch and go. I spent the whole summer in hospital and my leg was in traction. It was such a horrible experience and I felt it would never end. The recovery wasn't the best, but I put on a brave face. My mum must have been so exhausted during this time because she had to get the bus through to Aberdeen to visit me and with her work, my younger brother and everything else going on, I can't imagine how it must have impacted her.

My Academy years (11-16) were worse because I was out and about a bit more and the bullying got a lot worse, from the boys and the girls. The boys would mock me, my clothes, my mum (I hated that even more than what they said about me). They would beat me up and chase me just long enough for me to gasp desperately for air due to my poor fitness, but sometimes, instead of beating me they would laugh and remind me of how pathetic I was.

Some of the girls would be just as bad, there were a few who would come up and talk to me, pretend to be interested and ask me out. Once I made the awful mistake and said, "Aye, ok if, you're sure?" she burst out laughing and her friends (who were hiding round the corner) came out yelling things along the lines of "You f**king spaz, you think anyone would actually want to go out with you?" Looking back, I'm glad that mobile phones with the technology nowadays weren't around then. So as a result, even to this day I struggle to believe people when they complement me and especially when it comes to females. I really find it hard to see what they could possibly see in me. And as mentioned later, this belief gets reinforced many times.

When I left school, I was encouraged to get a trade of some kind, so I had more opportunities going forward. This is a standard wish for anyone's children. The main area of my work has always been industrial and engineering-based roles, so you can imagine the surprise of many around me when they find out about my spiritual side.

Initially I thought I wanted to be a mechanic but eventually, I got a job in a fish factory as an apprentice engineer. It was an experience to say the least. The fish wifies (women) were legendary in the kind of chat they had. Language that would make a soldier blush and a merciless humor to fill in their days. Of course, they would be the source of much of the town's scandal as a large part of the town's population were connected somehow to the fishing industry at that time.

One of the older and larger women pulled me into the toilet and said she would rape me. This was given as banter, but I was terrified, it took me a while to get used to that kind of humor because till that point, usually when someone threatened me, they actually meant it.

I was exposed to such a wide variety of people, and I couldn't handle it. I quickly pulled back and focused on my work until I could observe them more. I quickly learned what sarcasm was and how to use humor to avoid actually talking to people at length, it worked. So, I didn't make many strong bonds during my early working life.

The traumas being mainly repressed for now as I didn't know how else to deal with them, I developed (and hid quite convincingly) an eating disorder. I would obsess about exercise and what I was eating (or throwing up when nobody was around), I was also embarrassed about exercising initially so I would do push-ups and sit-ups in the bathroom. My mum and stepdad thought I was abusing myself in the eyes of the Lord. As there wasn't much in the way of mental health awareness, especially for men, my depression was generally met with "I wish you would just cheer up." And comments like, "What's wrong with your face now?"

Often, I would panic as I didn't want anyone to worry so I made extra effort to be a man and put on a brave face. I needed to create a façade, I started to develop a clownish personality where nothing was serious, and I went out of my way to be the life of the party. Again, this was done to keep people at a distance. But also, to distract myself from my own trauma.

As I got to 18 and started going out drinking, I struggled to make male friends because my interests were vastly different from most guys my age. But I made a couple of solid friends, Bob and Stan, who are still with me now.

During my weekend bar crawls, I was getting to meet females again. I was quite able to form friendships with them but there was always difficulty in getting any of them to start a relationship with me. I felt like I still wasn't good or thin enough for them. I dropped to around 10 stone (lightest I had been since I was about 10 probably) and wore baggy clothes to hide it. I discovered early what the friendzone was and it was so confusing and hurtful at that time. They would call me when it suited them to complain and then when they met someone else, I would be left to the side, until either they broke up and I was back in favor, or he did something terrible, and they needed someone to cry to. They would frequently ask why guys weren't all like me. It was a confusing time for me. I didn't want to be like those guys, but I didn't want to always just be a convenient friend.

I was an emotional wreck and at 18 I tried to end it all for the first time, thankfully I was very drunk and the cuts weren't deep enough to cause any issues or permanent scarring. However, there were some minor scars for a while and I had them covered up until, one day I forgot and my mum saw them. It was awful, but I couldn't explain anything and she couldn't listen. So, I had to man up once more.

It was around this time that Bob mentioned the gym and doing weight training. I tried it and fell in love. My eating disorder was replaced with an obsession to get bigger and stronger. I thought that if I was strong, people would respect me more. So, although I started eating and not throwing it up, I always saw the small fat kid in the mirror. I hated photos being taken of me, this is still a problem for me despite how my selfies might suggest and there aren't many photos of me during my late teens and early twenties. I would criticize myself so harshly. Although these characteristics seldom completely leave, I was eventually able to get them under control, but it was a long time before I managed it healthily. People would complement my progress at the gym, but I always assumed they were being sarcastic with me. It never occurred to me that they were being sincere.

My body confidence was (slightly) better as I started to see my abdomen tighten and my shoulders and arms develop so much that my t-shirts became quite tight in the right places. Physically I was separating myself from my peers and the positive reinforcement I felt I was getting on it was giving me some hope that I would be worthy of female attention. However, these changes were physical and not emotional and mental, it would be quite some time before I was able to start developing these areas properly.

There was one time I asked someone out, it was a mammoth effort encouraged by people around me. I worked part time at a local golden arched fast-food restaurant on the weekends to top up my low apprentice wages and I was especially fond of one girl. We got on great, would chat and sometimes hang out with others. I was at the drive through with some friends and asked her out (looking back I should have been on my own). She said yes (likely to not make me look like a dick in front of my friends as I was the driver at that point).

I was buzzing, told everyone I actually had a date and was getting so anxious on the days preceding it. I realized that I didn't know her address, so I found it out and bravely knocked on the door. Her mum answered and, looking surprised, informed me that she wasn't home. She stood me up, I challenged her when I saw her next but in my typical fashion, I made out like I was hurt and made it funny, so she didn't feel bad. She said she thought I wasn't serious because I was with my friends, so I asked again when we were on our own, she said yes once more. I really pushed the boat out this time and a guy with a carload of knock-off clothes stopped by my work so, following the advice of this man who seemingly had the knowledge of what impressed women, I bought a new (fake) designer ganzie (jumper in Doric) and size 32 jeans that were clearly not size 32 in an attempt to really impress her. And she stood me up again, her mum told me that she picked up a shift. I went to the restaurant to "get food for my family." To confront her again, she didn't even excuse herself, but complimented my ganzie. It wasn't a very pleasant experience and did nothing to fill my faith in women.

However, a twist of fate occurred one Christmas Eve, while I was content to watch E.T. the extra-terrestrial on TV and have a bath. Bob, Stan and a couple of other friends convinced me I was better off going out. Peer pressure has a way of changing your mind when you are generally agreeable. We bumped into her and one of her friends in one of the pubs (The Conti). I tried to play it cool, her friend seemed so disinterested in life and looked very moody. I don't recall the remainder of the night except staying at my pal Phil's flat and listened to him fail to impress the lassie (young woman) he took home. I crashed my car the following morning (nothing serious) and my stepdad came with his tractor and towed me out and I got a text from my friend Bob asking if he could pass my number on to the serial rejector. He thought something happened between us at last (he left early due to severe intoxication and inability to jive on the dance floor). I spent the rest of the day watching the 'Lord of the Rings, Return of the King' extended edition DVD in sections between Xmas dinner courses. That film is like 8 days long.

Anyway, it was her friend who was asking for my number, apparently, we connected in the Granada night club.

(Her friend eventually became my wife and mother of my children.) But before all that, I couldn't believe my luck. It took me the longest time to believe what was happening. This was an actual female who seemed to enjoy my company and not just to lean on when it suited her or to complain about her boyfriend, this time I WAS the boyfriend. I took all the lessons I had learned from listening to conversations and from the complaints of every female interaction I could remember and made sure she would never have reason to regret blessing me with her presence.

Looking back is always a wonderful thing, especially after a period of time has passed. The next 18 years were a mixed bag of me bottling things up and trying my hardest to be the best I could be. Don't misunderstand, I wasn't the easiest person to live with and the reasons why were explored later as I released things. I changed jobs frequently always looking for more, I never felt good enough for anything, so I was always pushing, seeking the validation from others. Yet never seeing when I had it. Always at the back of my mind was a need for answers, answers I wouldn't get, clarification that would never be enough and ultimately this relentless speed of life eventually caught up with me. And it was too much for those around me, I must have been such a nightmare to be around.

As you can imagine there were quite a few more traumas coming up for me, but those details aren't that relevant for now. The reason I have given some details here is so you can understand my fool's journey a little bit deeper and see the character development.

Taking the First Steps

My own interest in Tarot was built up from a love of games. Card games were a favorite of mine, I loved stats and comparing characters. Games such as Pokémon, Magic the Gathering and Dungeons and Dragons, which were filled with fantastic artwork and backstories, individually and collectively they really told a story about the cards. I could imagine the story of each character in the cards and how they would work in the game to compliment the multitude of other characters, items, and spells. My imagination was always on fire when I played with them. And I would spend hours upon hours poring over these cards and crafting the deck that I wanted to represent 'me' on the battlefield. Unfortunately, I didn't really have anyone to play with so I was putting all this effort into battles and scenarios that would be unlikely to ever unfold.

Because I spent a lot of my time alone, a passion developed for playing video games as well as these cards games, I found myself drifting in and out of focus as I preferred the fictional reality and wonderful characters and stories of games like Final Fantasy, Resident Evil and Broken Sword. They allowed me to explore character development and look at relationships from a safe place. Daily my own imagination became my comfort zone, role playing scenes from these games in my head where I was the characters I most related to, so I was always open to new ideas and distractions.

Reading was also an important part of my mental stimulation, authors like Christopher Pike and his love stories told through past life and alternate dimensions filled me with ideas of romance and hope that regardless of how other worldly the potential, it was entirely possible for true love to ascend and flourish. Terry Pratchett, with his fantastic worlds and humor gave me an appreciation for the ridiculous, the unexpected humor in things that otherwise would be ordinary and unassuming.

I would spend many classes daydreaming about these outlandish scenarios and loved the idea of being an author and storyteller.

Peterhead was predominantly focused on sports and physical activities or loitering around bus shelters smoking and drinking low cost/high content alcohol such as scrumpy jack or white lightning. I found myself being alone most of the time as I had no aptitude for either extreme. There was little interest in these types of games due to the "geek" status which was attached to it. Combined with the imagery of less than Christian figures such a monsters, demons, devils, and witches, it was not a popular pastime. Jump forward 25 years and "geeks" are now "cool" thanks in part to the exposure of such games in popular tv and film franchises.

Tarot was also a secret interest that I would occasionally hear about, and anytime I asked about it, I was left with the impression that it was not to be messed with, thought of along the same vein as the Ouija board and other tools of contacting the spirit world. Dangerous if used carelessly. My Grunny's partner bought a Tarot set of cards and everyone said the same things. That he had better be careful and they feared what could come from it. A couple of times I heard about my mum and Grunny going for readings, but it was very secretive.

As I explain the Tarot in more detail, it can indeed be dangerous if used carelessly as there is a great responsibility and trust placed on a Tarot reader, so we must be careful. Tarot lingered in the back of my mind, a tome of secrets and wisdom, only for the gifted few to navigate. Just waiting for the right moment to reveal itself to me. I was already a bit into my spiritual journey before I even considered the Tarot, but after a quick internet search for something unrelated, the Rider-Waite-Smith Tarot popped up as a suggested item. After some hesitation and silencing my ingrained protests that it was evil, I thought to myself. "Well, why not. If it's not for me then at least I tried it." I had heard of angel card readings and oracle readings so why are they ok but Tarot is not?

So that's the physical interest in Tarot. Now for the spiritual interest.

After a great many struggles with my mental health over the course of most of my life, the stigmas surrounding mental health were very constrictive, especially for men. So, I concealed these struggles until they burst out in the form of a breakdown starting around 2019 and culminating in 2021. I was already exploring radical (at least for Peterhead at the time) practices of meditation and other mindfulness techniques but these only got me so far. After almost 18 years together with the mother of my children (married 10 years), I made the heartbreaking decision to leave. There was a lot leading up to my departure, as I hadn't quite recovered from my breakdown and things were only getting worse, it was becoming more evident that I needed to change my situation. I was working down in Manchester for a few weeks, and it was the most time I had on my own in many years. Nightly I was drinking in the bars and finding that I was a different person with these people that didn't know me, I would talk to some friends and I would confide in my friend Angelica especially as she was the closest female friend I had and I needed her input from a woman's perspective, she didn't push me to anything but she gave her opinions and let me draw my own conclusions, I was not happy, I hadn't been happy for a while and it wouldn't change because I had asked, tried to speak and did everything I thought I could to change things.

Whenever I called, I could hear the disinterest in my wife's voice and it was obvious to me that she didn't want to talk. When I was home, I could feel her soul peeling a little bit more with every word I uttered. Understand that I don't blame her. I didn't make things easy, and I was in a bad mental state and didn't know how to get out of it. She would ask what she could do to help, and I couldn't answer. I feared my answers would hurt her, I needed some freedom, I needed to express myself and I felt I couldn't do it at home. This was highlighted when I was away. I was changing and heading towards a huge fall.

I felt an unseen hand at work, not so much gently guiding me towards something than hauling my ass out of there. It wasn't that I wanted to leave, but simply that we couldn't support each other anymore and we were both changing. The sound of the girls wailing as I broke the news remains in my ears, it was a sound of pure heartbreak. my guilt took such a long time to subside.

After an especially bad time for me following the breakup of my marriage and a plummeting descent into my own pit of despair, I was advised to try Reiki to settle me and help cope with my situation. My first impression of it was typical of those in my hometown and I shunned the idea at first. Even as I describe it to others, I basically place my hands on you, and you feel better. It doesn't sound convincing. But it works. So I went for a Reiki session and it literally, and I know how cheesy this sounds, changed my life. The statement, "You need to have the breakdown so you can have the breakthrough," is so true. It was the first real Tower moment (more on these later) I experienced. I had spent so long patching it up and maintaining it that nothing was holding it up when I fell.

From this new, more open view on life and the excitement that was associated with it, I explored spiritualism, energy healing, mental health, psychology studies and Metaphysics. I got involved in a Spiritualist church in Aberdeen who helped with mediumship development and during this time I was drawn to the cards. I bought a set from an online auction site for £6.50 (I have used the same set in over 1000 readings and they are still going strong) and it changed everything for me. When I finally had it through the post, I spent a long time just admiring the images and the nervousness I felt as I tried to comprehend all of what they meant. At first, I was afraid, (insert the lyrics from "I Will Survive") I understood why people were frightened of them but, I saw these magical cards as something with the ability to explain and guide almost anyone through, literally almost anything. But only if someone could interpret the beautiful images and find the story behind them. During my studies and practices with these cards I also invested in oracle cards to support my readings and add more context where required.

With my developing spiritual connection, I really felt the cards spoke to me in a way that other forms of divination didn't. With these tools, I could take people through their current situation, learn from the past and give them a not-too-distant future they could look forward to.

I cut my teeth with readings by giving them to friends and friends of friends until someone offered to PAY for the reading, as you can imagine this was something I didn't expect. I had always thought that the feedback and positive comments about the accuracy of my readings were just to avoid hurting my feelings. But this querent (person getting the reading) wanted to invest their hard-earned physical cash in my nervous reading. It was another life-changing moment because I finally had the beginnings of something I had struggled with my whole life, (despite how it might have appeared) self-belief and confidence. I was good at it, and I saw the potential for helping anyone who dared to ask for guidance.

From that point I have travelled around the UK and even internationally with my trusted £6.50 investment and offering Tarot readings in so many different situations and environments such as the back of shops, Pubs, cafes, Fayres and even in church halls (imagine the blasphemy). The people I have read for come from so many walks of life and one thing really started to become clear for me. EVERYONE has the same basic issues, from relationships, work, health, wealth too, what do I do and where do I go? I have had many unexpected experiences and stories unfold during my readings. And these are the references for this whole book.

We are going to explore what Tarot is, what a reading is, the psychology of the cards in general and what I have learned about life, the world and more importantly. MYSELF.

Chapter 2:
<u>General Terms</u>

The below terminology will help understand some of the references later.

Querent – Person seeking a reading.

Spread – The arrangement of cards during a reading.

Position – Each position in a spread will have different meanings. A basic example would be a 3-card spread from left to right. Past, Present and Future.

Upright – This would be the card laid down in a normal position facing the reader.

Reversal – If the card appears upside down facing the reader this is known as a reversal. This would change the meaning of a card and it could change the interpretation from potentially positive to a potential caution for the querent.

Blockage – This would be something preventing the querent from completing an objective.

Current energy – Would indicate how the querent is feeling or what they are dealing with in their life.

Dark night – A period of difficulty which could feel like despair or a very deep depression.

Tower moment – An event which shakes the foundations in someone's life.

Spirit animal and Totem – Our animal guides change depending on what we are dealing with, our Totem remains with us our whole life.

What is the Tarot

If you take them literally on appearance. The Tarot may be seen simply as a deck of cards which has some potentially triggering symbology. Taking a step beyond this initial thought and some may think that they have an idea of what the Tarot is. Some may think that it is the work of evil, some think it's a game. However, taking everything into consideration I believe it is best described as a tool, a very interesting tool that can be used for divination, guidance, to communicate with your spirit guides or just as something to change how you view a situation in your life.

People have a natural fascination with the future and anything which has the potential to give them a sneak peek at what's coming up so they can prepare accordingly, whether it's business or personal events. Not a lot of people will turn down that opportunity.

Of course, for many the first thing they might say at the suggestion of getting a reading is something along the lines of. "I'm scared, what if they tell me I'll die." Well sorry to break that bubble, but it happens to us all. It's how we react to death that will change how we view it. I have had people come with terminal illnesses and they have changed how the remainder of their life was led just by asking a few questions during a reading. I can't change your physical situation but I will try my best to guide your thoughts and emotions so your quality of life may improve.

When it comes to self-development, the benefits can be spiritual, physical, mental or emotional. Although there are some general terms and meanings allocated to each card there are many other potential meanings as there isn't exactly an in-depth instruction book which comes with them. It takes a great deal of effort and time to learn and build confidence working with these cards and even with some lessons, there is still much left to discover. Which is what makes it so exciting. Even after many readings, I still find that I am drawn to new and obscure little details in some of the cards and it blows my mind how it changes my view on them.

The symbols are varied as we examine each card and these can be as obvious as The Moon representing a cycle, The Empress indicating pregnancy or they can take a minute to analyze such as the spinning top on the Chariot which could mean balance through movement, the pillars next to the High Priestess which can represent Strength and Unity.

Even when it comes to some of the minor cards. Some literally have nothing to go on apart from the obvious situation like in the three of swords which is literally three swords piercing a heart which means that there has been a betrayal of some kind potentially with multiple parties to a busier card like the five of swords which represents conflict, but closer inspection of the clouds indicates movement and each character displays something different from the result of their efforts.

Regardless of how you view the Tarot currently, I assure you that your concepts of it will change as you progress through this book. Perhaps even tweaking your interest to explore it on your own terms.

History of the Tarot

Although the documented history of Tarot is over 500 years ago. Most history of the Tarot books normally begin with a statement along the lines of "The origins of the Tarot are shrouded in mystery." That instantly makes the Tarot more interesting. However, the most accepted history in a nutshell is generally the following.

The potentially first documented appearance was in 1392 by the treasurer of the French King Charles VI which recorded that three Tarot decks had been purchased. Legend however insinuates that it started as a card game long before this and was created in China and was the basis of the regular playing cards we have now: four suits with one suggested connection of (Cups being the Hearts, Pentacles being the Clubs, Swords being the Spades and Wands being the Diamonds) along with some court cards. Of course, there are many other connections with regular playing cards such as 52 being the weeks of the years, the suits being the four seasons etc. But let's not digress too much.

This then spread out from China and was brought to the attention of the knights of the crusade who brought it into mainland Europe, where the wealthy would commission cards to be made and displayed to guests.

From there the original 'Tarot de Marseille' was created and first used as a tool for divination by travelers. The notoriety increased in France when one of Napoleons Generals, Jean Baptiste Bernadotte sought out a reading from a well-known fortune teller and Tarot reader called Mademoiselle Lenormand (of whom a popular set of tarot cards is based on). He didn't want anyone to know who he was, so he created a false identity as a merchant looking for some business advice. However, The Knight of Swords uncovered that he was using a false identity as a merchant and not a military man, The Emperor was the second card and she spoke of Napolean who would become emperor and the third card being the King of Swords suggested that he himself would become a King, the final card was Death. These peculiar cards ultimately ended up leaving many questions for Bernadotte. The reading was bang on, and as history lay out, Napoleon was emperor, and following Napoleon's death Bernadotte revealed the reading a few years after the events occurred and he became King of Sweden.

The Tarot was kept hidden from the masses and only accessible through finding readers through luck as most of them were travelers. Some of these travelers had their own versions of the set and it wasn't until the late 19th century that the most recognized version of the Tarot was conceived. That being the Rider, Waite, Smith set. Instructed by Arthur Edward Waite, commissioned to the artist Pamela Colman Smith and published by the Rider company. This was instigated by the Hermetic order of the Golden Dawn and particularly by one of its most influential members Aleister Crowley whose own obsession with metaphysics and the spiritual realm are well documented. This is the prime reason as to why it is associated with evil. He also created his own versions and a set surrounding Thoth. Which was based around his beliefs about the ancient Egyptians and their connections to the Tarot.

The imagery and symbolism are no doubt influenced by his fascination with the macabre and the story followed a more consistent structure because of the collaboration between all parties. The set was completed and sent out for mass consumption in 1909. Since then, there have been literally millions of these sets sold and an abundance of replicas and other versions have been released while following the same basic structure.

Some of the cards were renamed, repositioned, and replaced as they saw fit. But this was the new standard of which Tarot would be measured, the fools' journey of the major arcana and the supporting 4 suits were to become some of the most controversial pack of cards in history. So that is why I focus on this set as my reference. If you can follow Rider, Waite, Smith Tarot, you can follow most other versions as well with little effort.

Other Decks and Oracle Cards

If I use other decks, which I normally do, I use them to provide filler details or to describe a personality. The varying images put a different spin on the same general meaning. This is something that only a skilled (high-five to me there) reader can do. To use so many sets (sometimes up to eight) and be able to fluently move from one to another can be very difficult. But it really gives a more rounded message to the querent and often cards will repeat which could really indicate that they should really pay attention to it in their life.

These other sets can be split into two categories: Other Tarot and Oracle. I'll explain them here.

Regardless of its imagery or theme, if something is described as Tarot. Celtic Tarot or Tarot of the Gnomes for example, it must contain at least the Major Arcana, that being the fool's journey. Some of these additional Tarot only contain the Major Arcana with no suits. There are different descriptions of course to suit the theme, for example the magician could be referred to as the Magi, Witch Doctor, or Sorcerer/Sorceress. The strength card could be might, power, or integrity. Despite these name changes, however they refer to the same general things, but the true meaning lies within the imagery on the card. That's the aspect of Tarot reading that takes time to build, anyone can memorize the basic meanings from the guidebook and for some that's enough, but - interpreting different images and relating it back to what has appeared before and after throughout the course of the reading is something that only the dedicated will learn. I have often found the meaning of the cards change based on additional cards coming out and information the querent shares with me.

The suits could be referred to as something else. Pentacles could be shields, coins, earth, or stones. But again, they share the same general meanings so it can be quick to interpret once familiarity builds.

Oracle cards, however, follow no specific format or structure. They are based on a theme, but each card is its own thing. Spirit animal oracle for example is focused on, well… the clue is in the name. But if a badger (I f*cking love badgers) appears, it's not to suggest he is on a journey to reach enlightenment. It is simply showing the animal's energy which is closest to the querents at that point in their life.

The first oracle deck I bought was a Faerie oracle. Each card is based on something to focus on mentally and physically such as being open to sharing and receiving information with elders. Be willing to accept help from a prince riding on unexpected frogs or just to spread your wings and GTFO of Dodge. Oracle cards are more direct with their messages, and it is up to the reader if they use the general wording on the card as enough to get the point across while interpreting the images, or they can use the guidebooks for a more in-depth explanation of the card.

Again, because of this basic format I find that they are very limiting for a full reading, so I generally use oracle cards to fill out the reading instead. But I may use them at the beginning to get souls messages for current energy, blockage, advice, and potential outcome and attach the tarot to these anchors.

Common oracle sets I use are Spirit Animals, Voice of the Soul and Prairie Majesty oracle. I also like using Nature's oracle from time to time to give the querent something to incorporate more into their life such as laughter, wonder, maintaining a childlike spirit and openness.

But there are literally oracle cards to fit any theme and purpose you can think of. Butterflies, angels, unicorns, emojis. They are far easier for people to create because literally, "this is something important for you to know", here is a picture of a gerbil in a fire uniform to reinforce it.

There isn't a story, it's like little inspirational memes thrown in to really add something special to a reading and I love using them to really hit home and give the querent something nice to take away with them.

Beginning The Fool's Journey

So, the basic premise of Tarot is the fool's journey from ignorance to spiritual and physical development and mastery of himself. It is a cycle which could also be thought of as different stages in life. We all go through many cycles during our life so if the World card comes out, it doesn't necessarily mean life is coming to an end, only that that part of life is moving forward (or backward) with the next step.

When I first started to learn Tarot, I was mainly using the basic guidebooks that came with the decks as reference. But often I found these lacking so much context and I was largely unfulfilled. I explored various online references, completed training courses, got readings from others, and watched videos of other readers to fine tune my understanding of the meanings and how to structure my own readings to best suit my ability as a storyteller. I took what I liked and didn't like from each of these sources and fine-tuned even further as I got more familiar with each image and the relationship between the others and even alternative meanings depending on the overview of the reading.

My passion grew and I talked about Tarot with anyone who was even remotely interested in listening to my laymen terms explanation of what it was.

Initially I would try and do my own cards and see how they turned out, but I wasn't sure if I was just trying to make the cards fit what I was wanting to see or if it was a genuine reading, so I decided early that I wouldn't read my own cards and placed a mental block on myself so I couldn't. During my first readings with friends, I was very nervous and because I wasn't familiar with the cards at that point so much of what I said was very unsure and broken. I needed a lot of prompting from the querent. Also, because I knew some of their situation it took a little while to determine if I was using my knowledge of them as bias on the cards. I was eventually able to separate this, but it took some time.

I spent more time learning the major arcana initially because it was very daunting to learn all the cards, but once I felt a little more comfortable, I tried to memorize meanings and orders of the suits. This proved to be very difficult, and I started to doubt myself, but then I found some short videos and other readings and found that they were taking a different approach to how other readers I met did.

They were a little more intuitive whereas the readers I had met till that point were a bit more focused on the general meanings and some of them even used the guidebooks to help them. I thought that was normal, but I didn't like it because I wanted my service to be more personal.

It didn't take too long for me to build some solid knowledge of the Tarot, and this started to show, my readings were mainly restricted to a few cards because I wasn't sure about how to structure a reading and it took me a long time to decipher the cards meanings.

Because I only had one set of cards to get me started, my readings were not complicated, and this was important as I had to fully learn them to provide the level of readings, I knew I could do. Over time people started to ask me to do short readings for them.

My first paying querent told me that my reading really helped him see things from a different point of view and he had some hope for the future because of it. I was thrilled and almost embarrassed to ask for a measly £10, but this was only the beginning. Part of my desire is to make myself available.

And affordable to everyone who might need me, so I have always kept my prices keen to ensure that they get value for their investment.

The Structure of Tarot

As mentioned earlier, Rider-Waite-Smith Tarot is the most known version, so this is the version I will cover. Most alternate versions of the Tarot follow the same basic structure, there are 22 Major arcana which form the challenges the fool must overcome in his journey.

There are four suits with 10 cards each (40 for easy math) which represent different aspects of the human condition and there are 16 court cards (four in each suit) which can represent people or characteristics in the querents life. Giving a total of 78 cards.

The readings can of course be structured however the reader decides, I have seen people separate the Major and Minor arcana to ensure that there are major events and minor events fairly represented. But this is based on how they prefer to do things. I will cover reading structures in a little more detail in a later chapter.

From here I will reference each section of the Tarot with a brief explanation and general meaning of each card. As mentioned before, this is not an in-depth look at the cards, just a general guide to common meanings.

Along with a personal part of my own journey and how I faced and overcame each obstacle. This will hopefully allow you to understand the placement of the cards in a larger life cycle.

Chapter 3:
<u>The Major Arcana</u>

<u>Major Arcana</u>

The Major Arcana is the main story of the Tarot, and it follows the fool from ignorance to enlightenment and includes all the obstacles he must face on his path.

The Fool's journey is one with many obstacles, he must take the beginners steps towards whatever it is he wants. From there he will encounter lessons and challenges that are there to develop and improve himself so he can thrive on his path and not perish from his efforts.

From taking the first steps and working through some physical, emotional, and spiritual hurdles such as creating an idea and making a hard decision to spending time in isolation. The Fool then delves deep into the underworld to confront the most wicked vices and blockages known to man. Emerging victorious he then develops clarity and a solid foundation to emerge a new man, complete and able to confront his initial hurdles with the skill, and experience to truly overcome them. The Fool's journey or cycle is representative of a major cycle in anyone's life and from start to finish these can be the same obstacles we each face as we work to improve our position in life.

The personal examples used to explain the major arcana begin when I first left my family and am struggling to find purpose in my life again.

The Fool – A man blissfully wandering, paying no heed to his surroundings and ignorant to the dangers. A dog is warning him of an upcoming hazard. Much like a child, the fool is curious and a blank slate for new knowledge, he is willing to go forward to learn and overcome obstacles. All his belongings are in a small satchel and he holds a flower, showing how ill prepared he is for more difficult times. The Fool is one who encounters a problem but isn't deterred by it. He trusts that what he needs will be available to him.

He is the first and last card, as he begins and completes his journey. This is a very powerful energy to appear in a reading, even more so depending on the position in the spread. For example, if he comes out as the present energy it could indicate that the querent is ready for a complete reset or fresh start. If it appears as a blockage, it could indicate that the querent lacks faith in themselves to act towards what they want. When I offer some potential meanings, many people say they are ready for a fresh start but, I am often met with blank stares as to what kind of fresh start it could indicate, much of the time it's because they haven't thought about it consciously, but instead it could be their higher self, preparing them for that movement. Unfortunately, as I will express with some other cards, many people get so stuck in their own rut that they can stay in this energy for the longest time. Change is scary and more so if there isn't a clear path for them to follow.

So now that I am the fool (insert self-deprecating joke) I am literally in a place unfamiliar to me.

During the first few weeks as a newly single entity, I was a complete mess. It was made clear to me by those around me that I was a fool (pun intended) for leaving the family. I was alone, for the first time in a long time, both physically and emotionally. I needed reasons, clarity, I would dwell on so much and had so much to say, but nobody to say it to. My mind would fixate on my phone while I waited for text messages that never came, prepared answers that would never be given and built frustrations that would never be sympathized with or absorbed. I tried talking and explaining things to my wife to no avail. What I thought I wanted was not available. I would later understand many things around these areas, but at that point I was still stuck in a depressed state so could only look at things from my own warped point of view.

So here I was, going through a whole transformation mentally and spiritually, I hadn't a clue what either of those things were at that point. I was working as a service engineer and although it wasn't a hugely challenging role, certain aspects of it were, I travelled a lot and this meant I had A LOT of time on my own with my thoughts, and as my work was in supermarkets. I saw all the alcohol offers and would often get gifted a bottle of something for going above and beyond to help the stores get their bakery machinery back up and running, so I would drink nightly, often to heavy intoxication. There were multiple occasions where I would be on the top of an industrial oven just weeping to myself because I felt I had nothing else going on for me, I couldn't be a father, a husband, or a man. What was left for me if not those things? Truly I had failed at life, so why continue to suffer it?

It was during these panic attacks that memories of some of the abuses revealed themselves to me again. I was so angry and at first, I refused to accept it, I convinced myself it didn't happen, and I was a liar. But these memories were so raw, and it was a true reliving of the fear and pain that really allowed me to finally accept it. I built up the courage to tell some people, I had hoped it would give them some answers for some of my behaviors and they could support me through this, I was mistaken. I didn't get the reaction I was praying for, and I felt even more isolated because of it. Disgust filled my heart as I justified to myself that I deserved everything that happened to me, and I had no business trying to put it on anyone else. I blamed myself for opening up about my mental health struggles, for ruining my life and the opinion of everyone around me. I imagined how disgusting and pathetic I must have appeared to them.

My mind was in such a horrible, twisted place. I called it "The Pit" one night while blind drunk and having taken some drugs I was quite easily able to procure. I paced the large, empty, silent flat. The memories of the past, the lost future, and haunting echo of my girls' wails repeating in my mind. I had reached my limit, there was nothing more I could offer anyone, everything was gone, my despair reached a crescendo and I survived what would have been at that point the first attempt since I was 18 to end my life, thankfully my body fought back and the thought of my beautiful daughters kept me alive. The bathroom was a mess however, bottles, pills, sickness, bubble bath and scented candles were everywhere. I planned to go out in my favorite place, the bath. (Honestly, I spend an unhealthy amount of money on bath products and candles).

After this there was an evening where, heavily intoxicated, I reached out to my mum for help and I unfairly released a lifetime of frustration at her, it was not my finest moment, and this created a massive wedge in our relationship, one that has diminished but it is still there. People say and do some very nasty things when they are not themselves mentally, that's a part that many cannot understand and accept, never mind offer forgiveness unless they have been there themselves. All they can see is someone they know acting irrationally. They can barely comprehend that the person driving the body is not the same, they are ill. That's an area of mental health support that should be explored further, how to support those suffering. Not just the traditional methods of therapy and medication which are mainly there for the patient but some actual support for the supporters would make a huge difference in people opening up and releasing trauma.

It was a very dark time for me and as time went on, my work suffered, and I had to do something about it.

One thing I still hadn't realized was that it was my own fault I was in that headspace, dealing with repressed memories haunting my dreams, panic attacks several times a week and over time I did start to settle. Eventually it dawned on me that I could go anywhere, do anything and experience what I want. But the main problem was, I had no f*cking clue who I was anymore.

After a lifetime of being fluid to the needs and expectations of others this was a situation that was completely alien to me. What did I want? Who was I? I mentioned earlier about the suggestion to try Reiki from friends, one of whom was a very special woman called Veronica who popped in and out of my life periodically. She was like the female version of me in a lot of respects. She had a keen imagination and willingness to learn but most of all, she was completely open to new ideas.

Unfortunately, she was battling cancer of various kinds yet despite this she was strong as f*ck. She was a real firecracker of personality, a truly beautiful soul. If the suggestion came from anyone else, I probably wouldn't have even tried it.

I was able to secure a Reiki appointment a couple of weeks down the line and although it was very hard for me to wait, I was able to survive with myself until then as the potential reset from the treatment kept me going. I wasn't sure what to expect but I knew this was the last chance I had. If this didn't work, I highly doubt I would have survived the new year. My expectations were so high. I didn't want it to work, I NEEDED it to work. And thank the divine father, for it did.

The true beginning of this path was after my Reiki session, I walked away feeling like a switch went off inside me. I had a feeling that I didn't know was possible, it was peace, my mind was so quiet, and my life energy was flowing without obstruction, anything could have happened around me at that point and I would have just accepted it and smiled gratefully. I felt like I could take on the world, I could see that I had a future. I just couldn't picture it at that moment.

The following few days were very settled and as I rebalanced from the treatment I could finally think with some sort of clarity. My work improved and I still drank but it was not so severe. It was still something I had to deal with, but the embers in my spirit started to flicker back into life. I had a purpose once again.

THE MAGICIAN.

The Magician – He stands before his alter, the tools available for him to create something, A true master of the elements, the infinity loop above his head shows a divinely intuitive mind. He points to the sky and ground indicating balance between the physical and the spiritual, "as above, so below." The four suits are represented here as well as some growth around the card, indicating the potential a good idea has. He doesn't create physical objects; however, he is a creator of thoughts, the spark of inspiration required to set an event in motion. The very earliest stage of an event.

The first challenge for the fool is the magician, who has access to all the tools required to manifest and create anything he wants. It's this character who inspires thoughts and ideas. Once the magician pops out it's a sign that the querent is ready to move but they are still looking for that spark of inspiration to choose a direction. He could also indicate a ritual or a manipulative energy if he is in a reverse position. This is a great card to start exploring other areas in the querent's life as they could potentially give you something to go on and form some clarification cards to fill in the reading and help guide them towards a situation. What's normal when I encounter the Magician in a reading is that the querent gets very frustrated with themselves because they feel ready for a change but don't have the capacity to plan and decide on exactly what it is they want to change. At times the magician will appear without the fool, this could be due to the querent having recently made a big choice such as leaving their job, without having another one lined up.

Now that I am a wandering fool with a fresh experience of energy healing, I was an open pot for almost anything to be placed inside and mixed around.

Fortunately, (or unfortunately depending on how you look at it) my desire to love and be loved led me to join online dating. I hated being on my own. Finally, and shockingly (for me) I had met someone. She lived in Dundee, and I was staying in Fraserburgh at the time, so we chatted for a few days just because it felt natural, we had banter and got each other's pop culture references, our situations were similar and were both nervous about meeting people in the future. So, we decided to have a date without any pressures or expectation, it was just going to be a one off so we each could get some experience dating again. Her situation was like mine, just with the roles reversed, so we had a lot in common. It was electric, we clicked instantly, and it was like we had loads of dates in one, we had a drink, went for food, a walk, a coffee, and a club for dancing. It took us both by surprise and we started dating more regularly.

We would talk nightly, share our days, and explore our pasts and what we hoped our futures would look like. It was real romance, we met regularly in Aberdeen as this was halfway between us and every time felt like the first time. The way she looked at me, touched me and held me was unlike anything I had experienced before. It was exhilarating. It wasn't out of convenience, or familiarity or because she felt she had to. It was because she wanted to. Was this true love?

We spent Christmas together with Veronica and her husband David and we all got on great. She was very much like me in a lot of respects. I really saw potential here and I imagined that this was what a relationship was meant to feel like.

But she cheated on me barely two days after Christmas. One of her friends contacted me during the night and told me how she was and what she was doing. She casually confessed as if she had innocently asked someone for the time. I felt the familiar sting of disappointment and rejection once again. Who was I to kid myself that I was ever going to be worthy enough of anyone again? I was a broken soul desperate for love I was kidding myself it would be available for me. But this time my mind changed its direction.

Something changed, I didn't go down that familiar path of self-hatred and doubt. I knew what I was and how I had value and potential for love. This time I wanted to find out why. We talked and as we did, she was more cut up about it than I was. It was because she feared the feelings she was developing so soon after her own marriage broke up, so her fears drove an impulse to reject the situation. It was clear that neither of us were ready for anything serious.

It was the first time I had really thought about things from someone else's perspective, and it was nothing personal. We separated for a while but remained in contact because I felt there was more to learn from our connection.

I was left with many choices as to where I went and what I did. As I explored my mental state from a different perspective, I began to understand certain things. I studied some free psychology lessons and mental health resources. I found some of them to be very lacking in terms of how to deal with things, especially from the point of view of someone trying to support a loved one suffering.

So, with my background as a trainer and self-proclaimed expert communicator, I delved into the world of live streaming on social media. Now there were already some people creating content about mental health, but I felt these were surface level at best, along the lines of someone prancing in some wood with positive buzzwords on screen. I wanted to be different, my content had to have depth. Something slower and more intentional to draw out the short attention spans of people on social media. No buzzwords, lights or jumping music. A break in the chain to break their mindless focus. I started doing 'morning motivationals' where I would talk for around 15 minutes about something positive like a film quote, talk about some mindfulness techniques and post a song which had a powerful message. Then twice a week I would do a deep dive into something affecting mental health.

The topics were either suggested by followers or based on something I observed: dating, gender politics, left and right-wing politics, work, money, communities, suicide, communication. Anything I felt was related to mental health I would look at, share my opinions, give facts, links for more information and speak about what we could all do to try and improve things.

Because I used a lot of my own life and experiences as reference, as I engaged with people and researched, I learned a lot, and this sometimes would be reflected during the videos. I wanted to share ideas with people in a safe way and let them see that there was nothing to be ashamed of by sharing their stories.

The videos were generally well received, and I got a buzz about getting this positive reinforcement. People I didn't know, some who I lost contact with, and others would reach out and tell me their stories and it was such a privilege, they would encourage me to keep going and tell me how brave I was for doing what I was doing.

But many close to me didn't like how I was exposing myself in this fashion, again the Peterhead mentality was that we should keep our secrets and not give anything out to gossip mongers. They feared how it reflected on them and this was very triggering for some. Although I was very careful with my words and especially from the point of being in a mentally challenged state, I would use things I thought and said to others as examples. Some did not see it that way and felt I was attacking and blaming them. During this period, I separated myself from a lot of people. It was my mindset at that point that if people got offended by what I was doing it was their issue, not mine. If they were triggered, it was because of an internal issue that they projected onto me. My intentions were pure, and friends and family were not spared the cull. I had to do this on my own. The tools of technology helped me to push and pull things on my table so I could then draw my path.

Since then, I have been able to think about and appreciate how this might have been perceived by others with much more clarity, but part of my content was created from a place of anger. I felt I hadn't been heard my whole life; this was my way of being heard. I was looking for a reaction. The conversations and answers I wanted were not being presented and one of my agenda was to instigate retaliation from some of those I was secretly targeting. It was a period that shaped my future but, had I the insight and understanding I have now, I wouldn't repeat these mistakes. It was an important lesson for me. I have since made peace and given apologies to those affected.

I knew I had to help people, but exactly how was I to do that? A podcast? A book? Coaching? I wasn't sure. But what I did know was that I had a hell of a lot to learn before I could do that. I don't like preaching what I don't practice, and I wouldn't teach something I had no experience or education in, so I began looking at other sources to get those two elements of competence: Experience and Education.

The engagement I was having with people who liked my videos gave me a lot of ideas. I spent most of my days planning my videos and this proved to be a great distraction. Unknown to me at the time was how they would be the building blocks of other things that were coming my way. What I was doing worked, I knew it was working and I knew I was good at it.

What I didn't realize was that by distracting myself, I wasn't dealing with my own issues properly and thus delaying the Tower moment to the point it would have caused more damage.

THE HIGH PRIESTESS

The High Priestess — She sits on her throne, confident and powerful, but not forceful. She controls the moon which represents secrets, a scroll of hidden knowledge partially concealed by her robes. The pillars of Solomon's temple represent Boaz and Jachin (Strength and Unity) and pomegranates decorate the curtain behind her, which conceals the future until certain criteria have been met.

She is the keeper of hidden knowledge and can help bring together and plan things going forward, she is the bridge between thought and action. Often when she appears the querent has some idea of the type of thing they want to work towards but is still not quite ready to take that first step. She normally incites excitement in a reading because it is an indication that the querent is going to start to see some potential outcomes down the line, they are the planning stages, and this is often the most exciting part of the process because you are not yet limited by physical or mental barriers. I love hearing about all their plans because you really feel the passion burning with some people. These plans have been anything from building a new house, changing career, or ending a relationship and starting over. It's wild the type of things that come up.

There was one reading that gives me endless mirth. There was a woman around 30 years old, reasonably normal and the reading was pretty standard. She was concerned about her work and romantic life. As the reading progressed, I suggested she could be focused more on her work for happiness because it would limit her time for a relationship if she wanted to grow both at the same time. As we drew more cards it looked more like she would set out on her own for work and this would eventually lead to a relationship because of that. She was thrilled with that prospect.

Then, the High Priestess made a shock appearance. I explained about her ability to plan and record tasks and instructions. She squealed with delight and proceeded to tell me about something she was working on. It turns out that she was OBSESSED with the musician Shakin Stevens. I nearly choked when she told me this because I wasn't expecting it. (Don't get me wrong, Shakey has the most elite Christmas song out there but that's as far as my obsession goes with him.)

She was actually writing a book about him. She told me about how she sat at a lake and meditated on all things Shakin, and she put mind to pen and pen to paper. I asked her to send me a finished manuscript. (Not received as yet but I remain hopeful.) I thought this was an amazing thing for her to reveal because although I found it humorous because of how unexpected and intimate it was for her, I admired her passion and sense of duty towards it. I have rarely seen that level of enthusiasm in anyone.

In my head she imagined her romantic connection would have led to a Shakey awakening but regardless, she was buzzing afterwards. And this is why I do it, she got a renewed hope in life and a burst of energy to continue working on herself. Every so often I think about that reading and how much it caught me by surprise, and yes, I always laugh.

At that time, I was still largely in a place of chaos, although I was leaving it. There were still lingering elements such as drinking more alcohol nightly than I should have been, poisoning my mind with intrusive thoughts and going round a mental 'less-than-merry-go-round'. I had to deal with the demons if I was to lead by example. After being introduced to some others within the spiritual community I had exposure to different aspects of holistic therapies such as hypnotherapy, inner child healing and alternative styles of Reiki.

Each new experience thrilled me with the possibilities of further enlightenment, but I had no focus yet on what that was. I started to buy crystals and meditate more; I did yoga each morning and had a solid routine built up. This was important because it gave me purpose each day.

Many people suggested that I got trained in some of these areas, so I started to ponder this. Previously when I was in the midst of my breakdown, I was looking for a new path and happened upon dream interpretation, past life regression and other types of alternate therapy courses. I suggested exploring this to my wife and it wasn't met with enthusiasm then, so I shelved the idea. So, with the suggestion it caused me to revisit these resources.

This was a more practical potential way for me to help others than merely through a screen, I could get out there and connect in a beautiful way. The wonderful experience I had with Reiki; I could give that to others. Eventually I did my Reiki 1 training for the first time and began working on my case studies. I was very close with Veronica and David at this point, sharing ideas on things like karma, crystals, past lives, alternative and natural medication, and reincarnation. She was the first person I wanted to try working on, she accepted and the feedback she gave me was amazing, valuable and it was such a healing, beautiful session.

She was in great shape and spirit. She was an anchor for me during this whole difficult period and she openly mentioned the positive changes she saw in me every time we met. She gave me the idea and encouragement to become a spiritual healer, for the first time I felt I had a potential vocation. Something I was passionate about and saw the overwhelming benefits for anyone open enough to give it a try.

The woman I was still in limited contact with after the Christmas betrayal revealed to me during this time that she needed me in her life. She wanted to redeem herself and she was so regretful about what happened. I believed her, we met for a second first date and after a lot of groveling from her, talking for hours and walking into the clear night, I really set boundaries. I shook off my remaining doubts and I thought we were going to be together for a long time. So, to make things easier I made the decision to move to Aberdeen to be closer to her, better positioned for my work but not too far from my girls. It was also away from the Peterhead area, and it could be a fresh start. I initially held myself back for fear of being made a fool (pun intentionally repeated) once again. If she was genuine with her patience and desire to share her life with me, she was going to have to earn it.

There were friends close by, specifically Angelica, who was a colleague of mine years before and was still around as a friend. We grew closer during this time as well and we really helped each other stabilize and sort our lives out. Her life was in a bit of freefall at that time, and we bonded like brother and sister. She encouraged me not to turn my back on this new path that I had wandered on to. Outside of Veronica and David, it was Angelica who mainly kept me in check day to day.

There were other new people around my life at this point who helped shape me going forward but I'm not incorporating other factors that are not directly related to this path. You will need to wait for my full autobiography for the filler details. Anyway, at that point I was still working as a service engineer repairing bakery and catering equipment in supermarkets.

Daily I would update the videos and pages with positive content. The supermarkets and towns, villages, and cities I would travel to with work were a hot bed of potential souls I could connect to. Everyone I engaged with was interested in what I had to say, and my following grew.

Comments, emails, phone calls. I was so busy with helping others that I was overwhelmed. Some reached out with advice to watch myself for energy vampires and users who would drain me, but I paid no heed (big mistake, as you will find out later). I was cocky and over enthusiastic.

I was ready to start shaping things into something tangible. I had been doing a lot of meditations and joining small gatherings and workshops to learn more, this led to some shamanism, and I discovered my spirit totem is the Bear. He is red and called Peter. This didn't really surprise me because I have been known as 'Andy Bear' in some circles for many years due to my generosity with giving of hugs (Bosies in local speak) and my general size and shape apparently makes people think of a bear when they meet me. These new discoveries filled me with excitement and highlighted even more layers to uncover on my mission of self-discovery.

Behind my left ear is a small tattoo of a Bear Pawprint with scratch marks in the colors of Red, Green and Purple which are the birth colors of myself and my two daughters. I also started wearing crystal bracelets and had stopped hiding my alternate beliefs anymore in public.

I was embracing this new path and was fully open to any and all suggestions for how to develop further. Part of me was distracted by this newfound energy but part of me was aware that I wasn't in control. There was a passive idea that I was headed for a crash unless I changed myself to compensate.

A chance encounter with a part-time counter assistant would provide that change and, in many ways, alter my path completely.

THE EMPRESS.

The Empress – She sits in comfort with her back supported, a crown of stars and precious accessories. She is likely pregnant and growing new life, there are many resources available to her as she has nurtured her environment. She is the feminine energy represented here and can help create opportunities out of nothing. Although very gentle and in good status, she is powerful and can impact any situation.

The sign of new growth, life and abundance, The Empress is an amazing energy because this is the beginning of the actual journey. The ideas have been crafted and shaped, the plans made and absorbed, action is finally happening and the querent has something tangible to hold on to. It could still be early enough for them to turn back, and this can indicate that is the case if she comes up in reverse. After planning and thinking and overthinking about it the querent can return to the fool's position quite easily as there hasn't been that much movement. Many in fact do this and often the querent opens with excuses and reasons why it wasn't right. Sometimes they are quite convincing but often it is because they don't like having their comfort zone stretched.

Normally when I mention the possibility of a pregnancy it is met with horror, but once I explain the potential new beginnings and lease of life the querent often can let themselves relax.

"You are one of us," a soft voice declared as I was signing the visitors' log in one of my regular sites in Aberdeen. I looked up and a middle-aged smiling woman who I had never seen before stalked over to me tentatively and deliberately, as if she was approaching a frightened deer. Her name was Becca, and she noticed the tattoo and bracelets. She told me she was a medium and involved with a spiritualist church in Aberdeen who ran a spiritual development circle, and they were always ready to welcome new souls.

It sounded too good to be true. Were there really more people like me out there? People who would welcome me into their circle and nurture me as I needed. In THIS part of the world? Mediumship had never even registered as a possibility for me because I was too focused on the healing side of things, but this would potentially help me get my energy under control and even provide some answers.

As I had recently moved to Aberdeen, I thought to myself, "What the hell, saves drinking alone on a Tuesday night." So, Angelica and I went along to a different public session where the developing mediums were working the platform (stage), and we could spectate and maybe get a message. I didn't receive a message but watching how they interacted with the crowd and communicated with spirit really got me interested in this. I had been to some audiences with a medium years prior but it just didn't resonate with me then. Obviously, things were different now because I was different. The energy I felt in the church was very loving and had a cleansing effect. Upon speaking to some of the members I attended the beginners' circle, and I found a group of people all in different stages of development but all together as one. Some were looking for healing, some for clarity, others to become a working medium. But I was there to find my reasons, my reason for living and reason for going through what I went through.

It was a wonderful experience, and I met some amazing people through the church. I still attend when I can. I felt I had found my flock. We shared things in a safe environment and grew together. I told them things I hadn't told anyone before and I wasn't judged, criticized, or made to feel like I didn't belong. Had I found my soul family?

Here I was exposed to divination and other forms of spiritual guidance like tea leaf and wax melt readings. But it was the cards I loved, different decks and styles. Channeling through these cards was something new and exciting, yet familiar and natural. It was an important part of my week and its impact really helped settle me from the chaos that, although subsiding, still had an impact in my life. Most of the group didn't like working with cards but I loved it. I left each week with something new. I loved sharing this with Veronica who really fed into it with her enthusiasm. I started to feel like I was becoming something else. I also completed my Reiki 1 case studies and was feeling like I could have a meaningful impact on the lives of others.

I was trying lots of different things during this time to find my main thing, areas like Shamanism, Paganism, Buddhism and eventually I stumbled across sound therapy. I had always loved music and sounds - I even tried to sing and play guitar in some of my videos. I was still creating daily content on social media and growing a steady fan base with some videos getting over 10,000 views. I pictured myself quite the sensation.

My belief at that point was that I would become an ambassador for mental health and be recognized as an influencer, doing motivational talks for people, and sharing my story to inspire them to try and understand the issues, not only around mental health, but how to support someone during a hard time. I was pulling from my own experience in opening up, and how I felt that it was the worst thing I had done because of how it alienated me from everyone. It wasn't anyone's fault, and I don't blame them for it. It was just a different world from where we are now.

My relationship was going from strength to strength as well. She really loved how in-tune I was with my feminine side and how I didn't let it overpower my masculine, we had a great chemistry which grew as we got more familiar and spent time together weekly. We even introduced each other to our own children. It was all coming together. I could really see how things were growing around me in a positive way. I also invested £6.50 in a life-changing set of cards.

THE EMPEROR.

The Emperor – A mighty figure sits atop a throne representing Ares, he has overcome great conflict and earned his place. The colors and barren background emphasize the struggles he has overcome.

He is the masculine energy, the logical part of a character, the stubborn energy at times which can lead to a situation going from good to bad due to an inability to adapt and bring on new ideas. This is a turbulent card that can potentially overshadow the empress and stop growth before it really starts.

The Emperor is a very strong, confident energy. Structure, discipline, and focus can be felt with him. But also order. If there is conflict around the querent the Emperor's energy is there to help overcome it. Depending on where he is in the spread, however, it can indicate a stubbornness to change and move forward or it can suggest a dominating masculine energy affecting the situation. This is a very straight forward card to come out, basically to give the querent a push to keep the momentum going.

I had someone come to me once for a reading and she did her own cards for a while but was getting nowhere. Before the reading she told me the Emperor kept appearing, but she couldn't place him. However, when he appeared in her reading with me it transpired that she was using an alternate version of the Tarot, so the images changed what message she got. Once I explained the card she instantly placed where he was in her situation.

I had decided early in my new life that I would do what I wanted with no regrets. I finally had some freedom to explore myself and I wasn't going to waste it. Having had an interest in music and wanting to create songs to inspire people, I completed a songwriting course I saw advertised. It was a free to attend certified course. I felt like this was a sign and something I could do. After spending some time on Zoom calls with my classmates and learning about their stories, my creative juices were truly flowing out of every pore I had. In fact, even before then, I would carry a notebook and write down lyrics and thoughts with the ideas of creating songs to uplift and understand my mental state. The course was valuable for my confidence because as with the spiritual and emotional areas, my music was never truly explored when I was younger.

Seeing as I still fancied myself as a future internet celebrity, I made some plans to pack everything up and follow my dreams.

As a matter of fact, when I was 18, I applied for a place to study guitar at Brighton so I could become a session musician. So studying music had always been locked in a small box at the back of my mind, overshadowed by other things and eventually swallowed by the mental clutter that accumulated. However, I unfortunately let myself get talked out of it. I blamed others for robbing me of that chance but have since realized that if I wanted it that bad, I would have committed to it then.

I didn't want to repeat that mistake so after submitting an audition tape and completing a rather intense panel interview, I was accepted to study music at the Academy of Music in Edinburgh. I put an extended notice in at work and was planning my future as a musician. However, as is standard in life, during these few months several big things happened.

While driving home from a supermarket in Arbroath, I received a call from a recruiter about a very well-paid job as a technical trainer; it was an area where I could have been considered an industry expert - instrumentation fittings and joint integrity. Initially I knocked the idea back as I was committed to my music at that point, however he persuaded me to at least go for an interview. It did seem as if it was too good of an opportunity to pass on.

The interview went well, in fact I would say it was up there with my best. My prep was on point, and I even had work samples to support my case for being the only option for them. They made the offer that same evening and gave me exactly what I asked for.

After considering this new position and how it could affect my plans, I felt it was the universe rewarding me for taking a risk by putting my notice in to study and getting the ball rolling towards a new life. Which was taking a massive chance on me and truly believing I would commit to change. Besides, I could use the extra money to increase my position and give me something to invest in my future - I could either work part time or save money so I could study in the future with less of a financial burden.

Outside of the evenings spent with my romantic interest, most of my time had been spent on my own, or with those in the spiritual community. This workplace, however, would enable me to interact with more regular people once again, so I was able to maintain my ability to connect with people of different backgrounds. I accepted the position and withdrew my placement at college.

After discovering and researching it previously, I was able to have my first real experience with sound healing, which was very powerful and very emotional, I felt I had found my thing. I signed up to do some training as a sound healer and was still building my strength mentally and spiritually. This was a very turbulent period of change for me and really tested my resolve. My social media activity had to be reduced to a couple of videos per week, so I had stopped the daily videos as I felt they were too much of a distraction, and I felt its growth was limited. It was apparent to me that I had got everything I could from this type of outlet. There were too many other things pulling my energy and I needed to decide where to place my energy to grow.

But I felt things were starting to line up for me. I was doing some readings for people, which combined with Reiki my confidence was starting to build more each week. Veronica and David were building a new life as well, literally. They had started to work on building a cabin on some land where they could live self-sufficiently.

The small single room cabin they started with was amazing. It was a miniature sanctuary, and it had an extraordinary healing energy in it. I was really digging it. As I was becoming more in tune with energy and controlling it myself, I really saw how this place could help with Veronica's healing. She (as mentioned earlier) had been fighting cancer. Originally, she was given a 6-month maximum timeline. She was still going strong 6 years later. She was a few years younger than me (she was 32 at that time) and was still as beautiful as she was in her early twenties.

She turned to alternative treatments, and it was working. Her love for life hadn't diminished, she and David got married the December before, so they had lots to look forward to. We talked about creating a fundraiser to get money together so she could get potentially life changing treatment in Mexico, and she asked me round to the cabin for a lunch with them. We chatted about many things, and we were all especially hopeful for the future. There seemed to be limitless possibilities and it was very motivating for me, she spoke of all the things she could see me doing and visions she had in her dreams and meditations, all of which seemed to center around me.

Her belief in me was like something I had never felt or experienced before. Everything I had ever done had been off my own back and I felt like I needed to really succeed before anyone would believe in me. Other endeavors I had tried in the past were written off as another phase by others, ideas I tried to share were met with rolled eyes and verbal scoffing. Thinking back, that might have been why I didn't stick to many of these projects. There is only so much you can do on your own. If those around you don't have your back, where is the incentive to keep going - especially if it was met with negative attitudes.

I remember that when I was training for a bodybuilding show it was a very lonely experience because nobody else understood or supported my efforts, I had no guide or backup so the whole experience was very negative for me. I would have arguments with others close to me because of the strict diet and increased time spent in the gym. I understood their frustrations, but this was a temporary situation, and they didn't try to understand why I was doing it. Or when I found there was a wrestling school in Aberdeen, I was urged not to do it for fear of embarrassment. Despite how much I wanted to, so this was the first time I had really experienced such genuine words and encouragement from someone for something I was truly passionate about, it was a wonderful sensation for me.

After lunch I offered to give her reiki while I was there. After setting up and cleansing the energy, I did my thing. The energy filled the room and was so dense and loving it affected the very air. It was such a powerful session that all three of us were floating at the end, all our spirit guides were present, and it was beautiful. After a slow recovery over several minutes and gently coming back into this dimension, we sat in silence for many more moments, contemplating all aspects of our lives. Past, present, and future. Unable to look each other in the eyes. The emotions were so high it felt like anything sudden would have sent either of us into a bout of tear-filled joy as we released some blockages. Both reinforced that it was my calling, they made me promise to keep going and improving.

THE HIEROPHANT

The Hierophant – As two monks ask for guidance, he offers mental clarity and advice on how to advance their situation. If he is preaching to the initiated, he finds new meanings and is confident with his suggestions. His feet are planted, indicating he is not one who acts. He prefers to maintain a neutral position and is more of an orator than a warrior.

Now that the querent is moving towards something they want, this energy is a guide of sorts, fine tuning the plan as they go and reshaping as required. This could mean that the querent needs, or is going to be giving, advice. Co-operation is something which might untap the solution. Like the Justice card later in the Major Arcana this could suggest legal or official proceedings to help with a resolution. If the situation is around work, this could hint at HR being involved.

The thing that I like most about the Hierophant is that he could be anyone, someone involved in the situation or not. It could be a stranger or a character in a film. This energy is one of guidance and that could come from any source, we just need to be open to it and pay attention. There have been many times I have been inspired by others to change my own situation and it has given me something to work on and improve. We need to think outside the box and adapt if we are to properly move on with our journey.

Less than a week later I got a call from David and a message from Veronica that she had been taken to Aberdeen hospital. She had had a few bad days, and they took her in for observation. I was shocked, as you can imagine, and my first thoughts were about the Reiki I did with her. Was it my fault? Did I set off a reaction by shifting something? I had to get these thoughts cleared because it couldn't have been my fault. She put my mind at ease when she said that she had been feeling poorly before and I shouldn't feel guilty.

When I went to visit, she looked so frail, but she was undeniably still Veronica, she was such a fighter. And the strength of her character shone through any tubes or monitors she was connected to. David stayed with me during the time she was there to save the long drives.

During my visit we talked about everything the past, life, lessons, regrets, the fundraiser, and the future. She had messaged me several times hinting that she knew her time was coming to an end because of how she was feeling. It was the first time she had really mentioned the end and I was trying to keep her positive. It was difficult to listen to her talking about her time in the hospital, she said she wrote a letter to the nurses asking them to kill her because she was in so much pain.

She asked me for a reading. It was short, and I was still learning the cards, but to this day I maintain that it was the most accurate reading I have ever done. It was like the world vanished around us and all that was left at the center was the two of us and the 3-card spread I had lain across her. Try as I might, I can't remember the cards pulled. The energy surrounding us was so pure and angelic it was one of the most powerful things I had experienced. She told me then that what I was doing was special and I needed to keep doing it and to share it with as many people as possible.

I thanked her and for the first time I started to believe her. I kissed her on the forehead and left; there was a look in her eyes I couldn't place at the time. She knew her situation wouldn't improve and that she was grateful to have had the experiences she did. Even in the depths of illness she had a good life, full of fun and her cheeky face and dimples were on full show despite the discomfort she was in. There was also a golden aura around her, a sign that she was being looked after at a higher level.

Had I known that was the last time I would see her I might have stayed longer, or at least said some things differently. She passed less than 2 weeks after that. The deterioration from then was so rapid they couldn't do anything; she spent her last couple of days with David and her parents where she enjoyed a gin and orange juice for the last time. I'm just grateful my last memories of her were while she was still Veronica. I will always look back and remember the look in her eyes, eventually I understood it was not fear or sadness. It was strength and gratitude.

Regardless, it f*cking broke me.

The funeral service was a beautiful and very fitting tribute to her life. Veronica saved my life and gave me more than love. She helped me rebuild my spirit and let me see that it was possible to enjoy life again. She had such a unique ability to help all around her, just by existing. She was truly a beautiful friend and soul.

Even as I write this, tears are falling onto my lap. She was such an important part of my life and although she didn't realize it, she was the guide I needed. If it were not for Veronica, if I was still here in this life, I would still be cursing under a bread plant in a supermarket somewhere, drinking every night to sleep and barely functioning day-to-day. I had lost a massive part of my life so as I recovered, I promised her that I would honor her wishes and get better. I would learn and help as many as possible.

She has come to me during meditations and spiritual work. I know she is still guiding me and every time she blesses me with her spirit, tears of joy line my eyes.

Since the funeral, David and I lost contact, as I was Veronica's friend to begin with, it must have been hard for him to maintain contact. He needed to recover and although I check in now and again, I respect his need for some distance from that part of his life.

For the other areas in my life at that point, the spiritual church was a big part of my routine, and I was developing nicely. Angelica and I were in contact almost daily checking in and keeping each other in balance. I had started working part time at a gym doing maintenance for extra money and a free membership as I had started to train my body more intensely now my confidence was improving, my relationship was still going well but cracks were starting to show, mainly because of all she had going on around her, her divorce, selling the marital home and moving. I was expecting something to happen as we had some troubles with communication, and she was struggling to cope with everything. However, I was prepared for what was coming because I had so many other things going on around me.

I felt the universe pushing me towards something else.

I completed my Reiki 2 and Sound therapist training and made the commitment to put myself out there. I stopped doing the videos altogether and decided to focus my energies on something with a little more meaning. I had a future to walk towards, but it was still a formless entity. I still had a strong idea that I wanted to help people with mental health issues, but the format was the aspect that still was missing.

As I became more at ease with speaking about my spiritual side, I found myself healing people at work and friends of theirs.

It was a great learning experience, and very important in familiarizing myself with the new levels of energy I had and how to use it to help.

The Lovers – Adam and Eve stand before a tree, each of which bears different fruit and flowers. A snake wraps itself around one. The angel can represent a hidden choice, wisdom or a third party observing the situation. The clouds can be thought of as a third option without having the clarity of the other 2. This is a choice which will shape the rest of the journey.

THE LOVERS.

This is one of the most well-known cards. The lovers can mean so much to everyone that is often hard to place. It is a choice, possibly between romantic connections, between a high risk/high reward or a low risk/low reward situation. It can be seen from above as if the querent is witnessing a situation unfold before making their decision. From a point of duality, it could be some conflict between the spiritual and physical aspects of a person.

I remember I was in a pub offering mini-readings for a shandy and a double rum and coke when a woman asked for one. There were a few things about a new dog that came up and a new beginning, BUT when the lovers came up in reverse, I suggested that she felt like she might have made a mistake in romance. Her face dropped like a solid fart on the bathroom floor. She looked

*around as if a drug deal was about to occur and pointed to a guy.
"That's my husband, we are on honeymoon, and I think I f*cked
up." It was hard not to laugh but I hope they were able to work
it out.*

After the passing of Veronica, and a few other things during the following months, my relationship ended. She had her own demons and she hurt me more than I would have let her know. Lies, unfaithfulness and paranoid accusations were among the hurtful things done to me. Looking back, although I felt it was coming, I should have seen the signs that we were not compatible earlier, but my desperation to be loved and lingering fear of never being enough led me to ignore these doubts. I felt like I still should have been grateful that someone would string me along for so long. My focus was also split between so many other things it caught me by surprise. As usual, I took the full brunt of the failure, I convinced myself that it was all my fault and I didn't match her expectations, this was why it ended. It took some time before I was able to come to some other conclusion. But when I did, I moved on pretty quickly.

But before then, with so much for me to process, all my emotions came out at once leading to a huge mental and spiritual crash. The drinking got worse, drinking every night and often full bottles of spirits were consumed. I was lonely and drained, and I really couldn't imagine a different outcome for me, I had lost something just as I started to grasp it. Life had seemingly reminded me that regardless of what I did and how hard I worked, it would never be enough, and I should take whatever small graces I could as more than I deserved and enjoy them while they lasted, I was only ever going to be a supporting actor in the stories of others. There for some comic relief or to advance their plot in a small way.

This is something called the "Dark Night of the Soul." It's different for everyone and can last more than a single night, but anytime you try and change something so ingrained in your character or challenge your core beliefs (or self-doubts in my case) the mind fights back. It doesn't like having its comfort zone challenged. After an exceptionally hard night of things, I wrote what I thought was going to be my final letter to my girls and whoever found me.

I tried calling the Samaritans to no answer and I took this as evidence that the world really didn't give two f*cks about me. As my stupor widened, I blacked out. I was awakened by the paramedics. Apparently, I called 999 and cried for help. The carpet was red, and I was in a mess of blood, suspected to have stemmed from an impact and broken glass, I must have lunged in anger over something. There were no pills this time and no cuts, paper was strewn across the floor with all kinds of things written down to whomever it was for. After calming me down, talking and cleaning me up they decided that I was no longer a danger to myself, gave me some phone numbers in case I needed to reach out in the future and they left. My respect for these emergency workers has always been high but after this event, it was elevated to the heavens.

I took some time off my work and really had a moment of clarity. I had released many things during this event, and I was ready to start again. I had conquered this dark night. With the tools, ideas, and commitment to plow on. I decided to make a serious go of things.

The training role was initially great and helped me to build myself up. But I was not fully focused on it, I chose to pull back from a few other areas, mainly finding romance and the spiritual work for now so I could recover. I had been involved in training for around 10 years by that point and I felt it was a great opportunity to really build back my confidence in dealing with people, so this didn't take too much effort from me. Of course, I had been doing my videos previously and was used to talking, however it had been some time since I had an actual audience. It would be something that would shape how I communicated with people going forward.

I went in balls deep; I was determined to start as I would go on and really let myself go. They were not ready for me at my maximum output, so I tamed it down (just a little bit).

It's amazing to think how much you can learn by delivering the same materials to different people. Some groups were experienced, and some were attending for the first time. I had to tailor the sessions to suit each group, and this was dynamic and at times difficult because I still had to be engaged, otherwise I would have lost their attention. It was important to think of different ways of explaining something to someone who is familiar with it, and you want them to gain something from the session or someone who has no clue what you are talking about. It was exciting. This was a skill that really helped refine my readings because every time a card comes out, depending on everything else, I might need to think outside the box to get the right point across. I need to invest the querent in their own reading and the best way to do that was by making sure they understand you are not giving them the same script as everyone else.

This is a point where I feel I really separate myself from many (not all) tarot readers because I have specifically developed my communication skills and storytelling abilities. My ability to think with more fluidity and explain things beyond the card's imagery and guidebooks, I can inspire and motivate people to get excited about overcoming their blockages. Because of this, people leave with the impression that it was more than just a reading, I was outlining their life and its possibilities as if it were more than just a suggestion. I go all out to invest people in their reading, and this is one thing that causes them to return.

Don't misunderstand, I am not suggesting I am the best reader on earth. Far from it, but I always go into each reading with the hope that I could get it right for the querent. I don't believe I am more than I am. My ego is detached from the reading so that I am not giving anything the querent doesn't need. What I would say is that I am a reader who has developed my skills both outside and inside of the cards.

I would 100% tell people that although they may receive a more accurate reading from another Tarot reader, I would also say that they would get the best reading I possibly can give them 100% of the time.

The Chariot – A man leaving familiar territory struggles to control the ? sphinxes. A spinning top represents movement and balance; the angel wings mean spiritual support and intuition. The stars, moon, and solar system are all represented on his armor and canopy. If he cannot control the chariot he will be running in circles and his journey will be difficult.

Once the choice has been made by the Lovers, the querent must handle the chariot to maintain focus and direction. They have left their safe place and security and chosen the path that is less travelled. But this is a card of balance as well, constantly remaining vigilant on the road ahead and not letting go of the reigns and releasing control to the 2 sphinxes which are pulling forward. I often refer to the 2 sphinxes as representing the spiritual and physical aspect of life. If you let either side dominate, you will end up going around in circles. Think, plan and act.

One evening I was waiting for a client to do some crystal reflexology and a very intoxicated young lad from Liverpool, *who was in Aberdeen for work, tottered in and asked me for a reading. It was my first walk in. The Chariot was a blockage for him, his reading was mainly concerned with love and with the support of several other cards like the 7 of swords and 4 of cups it was obvious he was not a faithful person. He was asking for another chance with his partner and, with the chariot being the blockage, I basically told him he had to think with his big head and not just his little one. He saw the funny side to this, and understood the general message that he really needed to prove himself to his (then ex) partner if he was to really deserve another chance. I haven't heard from him since so I am assuming the best. I sensed a misguided energy from him, but his heart was gentle. It was one of those readings that I expected to be really sh*te, but it turned out very positive and he left delighted. He even told me I didn't charge enough for what I gave him.*

The Chariot is the fastest energy in the deck, so when it appears expect rapid movements once its wheels begin to turn.

I decided to make a serious go of things. At any chance, I would speak about what I could offer and volunteer my services for free with the idea of generating buzz and word of mouth clients. Slowly, people would message me and invite me around because I was eager to please and wanted to give people value for money, my sessions were extraordinarily long. After reiki and a reading sometimes, I could spend around three or four hours with a client. It wasn't very sustainable and free time was already sparse with my working two jobs. Although I still don't time things as I don't like to rush or put that pressure on the querent to think they have no opportunity to ask questions or delve deeper into something, my structure and service are now more efficient and effective.

After some time, I created Bear Paw Holistics as a business to give me some credibility and let people see that I'm not just working in the shadows. It was a declaration of my intent and belief that if you trust me and pay me for a service, you will not regret it. I can help.

I took what little money I had and invested in tuning forks, singing bowls and everything else I needed to get going. I started to work the circuit doing markets and fayres, building my profile and networking with similar small businesses.

Something that was obvious to me after a while was that although I may not have made much money at these events, my table was always one of the busiest. My unique tools, general patter, and willingness to engage with everyone around me really drew people in and this led to me being asked to other events and bookings. I was getting more regular clients looking for healing and there was a buzz in particular around about my readings.

I want to see everyone succeed, so I generally didn't offer readings for people at the fayres - there were usually plenty of others doing that. So, I focused on what made me unique. I was normally the only sound therapist (I only actually met one other, Davina. More on her later), but over time people would ask me to offer readings as well. This was confusing for me at the time because my confidence was still growing, and I saw myself more as a healer than a reader. Initially I resisted this pull but not for long.

As the year progressed, someone invited me into their shop in Peterhead of all places to do readings for their customers. It was a nice experience and it made me think there was really a demand for what I offered. People started to talk and ask when I would be back up to take more bookings, others asked me round for group bookings and this gave me some confidence that there was potential for me to grow further.

The hands of fate worked and shortly after this the unit next door to the shop was advertised for rent. I started to think about creating a safe space, my hometown is a place which seriously needs healing. Initially, as you can appreciate, I was put off by the idea because I knew the risk of setting up in Peterhead. New businesses generally don't get welcomed into the town, never mind something as different as I was planning. 'But' if I cracked the nut, I would be on to a winner.

It really was a high risk but high reward situation. It was an old taxi office and needed a lot of work, but I'm quite a handy guy having spent most of my working life in workshops and fixing things. I had no money, but I was quite resourceful, so I thought about it, negotiated for a couple of months free rent to get the place set up and off I went. This was at the start of December. I had nothing to my name except a lot of romantic ideas about my future life as a healer, self-belief and a Facebook page with less than 50 followers, but here I was getting ready to "Heal the world, one soul at a time."

I endeavored to have the studio set up by new year. I was already working two jobs on top of the bookings I was taking. So, it was a rough time. Up at 0430 each morning to work as a maintenance man at a gym then start my day job at 0730 until around 1630. From there I was driving an hour to Peterhead to work on the studio, sometimes until well after midnight, driving back to Aberdeen to start again the next day sometimes (barely) sleeping in the studio so I could make the most of the weekends. I had a vision of what it would look like, and I made sure that if it didn't match that vision, I would have nobody to blame but myself. Over the course of December, I plugged away, often questioning what remaining sanity was still floating around in my mind.

By this point Angelica had started to see someone. He was a very jealous person who gave her a hard time being my friend (usual story). So I got removed quite sharply from her life. It hurt me so much and it would be a while before I grieved the loss of her in my life. So, I was alone once again, my friends Stan and Bob were still with me but with their work and general lack of interest in the spiritual side of things (it's not for everyone and I don't judge) meant there were few opportunities for us to hang out. I had to do this on my own.

For months following the breakup, and Angelica being out of my life I had been thinking about moving back to Peterhead to be closer to my girls as they didn't feel comfortable in the Aberdeen flat. But I didn't see them that often, so I put it off and tried to ignore the idea. But Bob was in Peterhead and Stan was still as close, so it made sense. The studio was the final deciding factor.

To this day I am not sure where I found that drive or motivation, but I was possessed. My hard work paid off, however. On December 31st, I had got to the point where I was happy with how the studio was looking and it was an exact image of what I had imagined. As I locked the door for the last time until the 7th of January when would I run my first public sound bath, I felt relief, emotion, and something new, pride. For the first time in my life I felt real pride in something I had done.

I had achieved things in the past by competing in bodybuilding, strongman, and powerlifting, although I didn't win these events. The participation and proving to myself I could do it was a victory for me.

However, this was something I imagined, worked on, and created and it was 100% my own achievement. I had taken control of my life and picked a direction. What I was to learn was that it's not just about creating it, I had to keep it moving forward.

My chariot was moving but only I could steer it. For the first time the outline of my future was solid. The fine details were not quite there but it had shape, it was a real thing and not just an idea.

STRENGTH.

Strength – A woman has subdued a lion, but not using physical strength, it was her strength of will and character that did it. Instead of fighting back the lion is co-operating willingly and is happy to do so. The infinite loop indicating her superior mental abilities and out of the box thinking is similar to the magician.

By using alternate methods to control a difficult situation the strength card can refer to the physical, mental, emotional or spiritual strength required to take control. This is a great energy as when it appears it is very clear that regardless of what imagined fears the querent has going forward they can be assured that they can handle it, often in ways they don't understand. This card is quite common in readings when the querent has some doubt in their mind about whether they can manage to keep up their current situation, or if they are using a lack of strength as a reason not to start. It is wonderful to see the expression change in someone when you can reinforce the message, "YOU GOT THIS", and convince them to go for it. If this card has a preferred place for me, it must be right at the end of a reading. At that point we have explored the current energies, the blockages, maybe even flicked a middle digit to the past. But all the talk and doubt vanish when this card comes out, and it is truly inspiring to see people believe that it is possible.

The first sound bath wasn't a rip-roaring success. Only a single person turned up and, to the time of writing, she hasn't come back, so it wasn't the start I had hoped for. However, I did expect growth to be slow and it wasn't a deterrent for me. Week by week and fayre by fayre I built my social media and attracted new followers and clients. I kept putting myself out there and yes, I was able to retain some regular clients, but it wasn't enough.

The people who came to see me regularly at the sound baths kept giving me amazing feedback and I saw a huge difference in them from when they first started coming to me, it was live feedback. No words had to be said, I saw and felt it in their energy. It was a place where I was able to fine tune my craft and structure, not only my sound baths, but I was able to work with some unique people for Tarot readings.

Some weeks I would only take in one client and the Sunday morning sound baths often only had one person coming along. I felt like I had failed. I put everything I had into the studio but some weeks I would question everything, and it was a very emotional time once again. Was I kidding myself with what I was doing? I knew it was something people needed and if they let it, would improve their life. After months of putting what little money I had spare into the studio I eventually had to give it up. This was a very hard thing for me to do, what would have been a massive setback for a previous version of myself.

I shared my story on my Facebook and local pages to explain once again what my intentions were and that I couldn't justify continuing. It took all I had not to break down as I pulled the window decals down and packed my things.

My final sound bath had two people. I was hoping for more after the messages of support and pleas not to give up. But these were only words, people are always quick to suggest or offer help but when it really counts, well, let's say till then I had yet to see them back up their words. I was heartbroken. As the attendees lay down and relaxed, I broke down inside barely holding back the tears as I sung my bowls and calmed them down with my instruments. I was fully preparing for another 'dark night.'

But instead of blaming everything on everyone else and getting drunk, I took it on the chin, was able to find a new tenant so I could get out of my lease and put my thinking hat on. I analyzed the whole thing to see where it went wrong. Firstly, I limited myself to only working when there was a booking, and the only thing that was consistent was my Sunday morning Sound Bath, so people didn't know I was open. Not everyone makes use of social media, so a lot of my posts were not getting seen. I also limited myself because I still worked full-time, so this had an impact on how available I was to people.

In addition to this was that I made myself limited to being in Peterhead. If you can cast your mind back to earlier in my story, I hinted at the reluctance of Peterhead to welcome new (especially different) things.

This idea was reinforced as more than a few people would check outside the studio before leaving to make sure nobody they knew saw them coming out and a lot of the engagement on my social media posts were not from locals.

Some of the local groups were also very reluctant to let me post on their pages or even allow me to do free sessions to share my work and help. I reached out to the local health groups and community meetings to promote holistic therapies and the benefits it could have for mental health, but the organizers didn't even pretend to be interested in anything which (in their opinion) didn't come from God.

So, I still had a lot of work to do. I needed to change myself and how I did things, I needed to tell the universe once more that I meant business. I wasn't going to let this deter me. I reduced my hours so I could make more time to build up, I started doing more markets and being more active on social media. I doubled down and changed how I promoted myself.

I was trying to put myself out there for Reiki and Sound healing, but it was always my readings that were the most popular. I decided to give the people what they wanted.

THE HERMIT.

The Hermit – He wanders around in the darkness alone, but this is his own choice. The lantern he holds contains a star, a symbol of clarity, and his staff could represent his energy. He takes his most basic elements and searches for a place to invest them. He is methodical in his search for his own way and his patience is something which will prove to serve him well.

The lone figure in this card is taking control of his own light and going where he wants, this is a period of deep contemplation as to where he has been, where he is going and if it still aligns with his purpose and goals. This could be a difficult situation because changing something at this point can set the querent back a few stages, although certainly not right to the beginning. They are learning how to adapt and maintain their course of action, which this is often the case when people are putting finishing touches on a project before the final push. It can be thought of as a point of no return. If they go on and it doesn't work out, they may as well start again. Often it can point towards someone coming into the situation to help shine light on something.

Many times, when the Hermit appears, the suggestion of pulling back is often met with various reasons and excuses from the querent as to why that's not possible. Being alone is difficult, and many people cannot make the choice to do this. Especially given how wired everyone is these days and addicted to instant stimulation and feedback, its like breaking an addiction to some to even consider having an hour without any internet or social media. Even though it would mean better things could be available to them by clearing their head and giving themselves the space, they need to refocus and centre their energy. This can often be the stumbling block for people in their journey.

During my planning and brainstorming I decided to make use of my skills and take a step back for a short time. I created a course in how to do your own tarot readings, attended events further afield to deliver talks and workshops on mental health and mindfulness and joined some networking groups to build my professional image. It was during one of these fayres that I met the only other Sound Healer in my local area, Davina. We were positioned next to one another during a very quiet Sunday wellness fayre. She was offering Reiki and I, Sound Healing. We hit it off. Although she was in her 60s, her energy was very youthful, and she was such an amazing character.

We shared details and chatted the whole day. Even though neither of us made any new clients, it wasn't a day wasted because over the coming months we helped each other tremendously.

I completed my Reiki training once more with Davina and became a Reiki Master. This was something I needed to do to really draw out my potential and enhance my energy work. The readings improved because of this 'spiritual power up.'

But I was still limiting myself to what was familiar. I pulled back my energy and distanced myself from distractions. I needed to really commit myself in a way I hadn't done before. I went back to the drawing board to really look at what I had done and how I had grown. Yes, it had been steady progress, this was time to step it up.

Eventually I decided to offer something a little different on my Facebook page. After watching some online tarot readers, I decided to put my own spin on them, add my own style of humor and posted online each month to attract people to my page and give people a way to check me out before making a booking.

It worked. I increased the page, got around a bit more and started doing sound baths in other locations. It was the rate of growth I needed before, but it still wasn't enough.

The training job was starting to become toxic. Not the job itself, rather the work environment. People really couldn't stand to see me so happy and positive all the time, couldn't understand me and so I experienced workplace bullying for the first time in 20 years. Staff were putting in false allegations and complaints about me on an almost weekly basis. It was such a heart-breaking experience because I felt like I literally couldn't speak to anyone.

I have always tried to be kind to others with my words and am especially aware of how I carry myself in conversation and with my body language. It was very difficult for me to remain in such an environment, so I withdrew, stopped speaking to everyone unless it was absolutely necessary, had my lunch alone and I noticed a huge difference in my sessions. People would openly comment on the shift in me and pretend like they were shocked when I would tell them why.

Delegates would look forward to my sessions because their colleagues had attended them previously so I had a great relationship with the trainees coming in and they would talk about the sessions at their work. I knew I was doing a great job. But when I wasn't in the classroom, I was a ghost. I was barely talking to anyone inside and outside of work and I really pulled back.

I wasn't having any luck romantically either. I had met a few women for dates and was left largely disappointed because of cat fishes (people who look absolutely nothing like their picture, so in my mind that is a lie and is a sign of someone who is not genuine), poor compatibility, and the fact that the online dating scene is one of the most toxic and damaging things we have allowed to develop in our society. I honestly think it has ruined relationships for at least two generations. This was another area which I decided to pull back from.

I examined every part of my life and tried to see where they fit in with my higher goal and desires going forward. It was quite difficult to be objective and not be stressed out about my financial situation.

The woman who I thought I had a future with reconnected with me; she wanted a way of apologizing. We chatted and met up a few times as friends. I was very lonely, and I didn't care about the past. I just wanted to be with someone. I had hoped there was still something there. Until then, nobody had looked at me the way she did. Was it true love? After a short while she asked me to move in with her to Dundee so we could make a serious go of our relationship. I thought about it and eventually I said yes, still convinced I was lucky to have anyone interested in me, despite what had gone on before. I felt grateful to even have the chance again. I believed she had made some mental improvements since our last encounter.

However, as seems to be usual for me, it wasn't that simple. Turns out she still had lots of issues, but I wanted to help.

We made plans for me to move in with her for a few months to see how we got on and how her children handled it before making serious plans to get a place to stay which was better suited. Perhaps my new life was in Dundee. I reached out to a few people I knew around that area from within the spiritual community and started to plan my new life. Peterhead truly had nothing for me, and I wanted to leave as soon as I could.

I found some new tenants for the flat I was renting and was preparing everything else. I left my work to find employment closer to Dundee.

But, and there is always a BUT. She changed her mind, after all the pleading for another chance and begging for me to move in with her, she withdrew at the last possible moment. I didn't see it coming and although I didn't fully let my guard down, I still felt like such a dick.

Everything around me was so draining. I was in a worse position each month financially, I had nowhere to live and no job.

My personal situation was worse than ever because, outside of work, I would speak to no-one. My relationship with my family was in tatters and unlikely to improve, my children were too busy and preferred not to spend time with me. They were coming to an age where I wasn't cool, so I understood, and I tried not to take it personally. Because of my beliefs and barriers, I had removed almost everyone around me to protect my heart, but I was so painfully alone. So, I made some pretty drastic choices in a very short space of time.

If I was headed down I would do it my way. Never one to do things by halves, I packed my sh*t and went.

WHEEL of FORTUNE.

Wheel of Fortune – The great wheels can be thought of as the end of the physical part of the fool's journey as it relates to the 10s in the suits. (my opinion). The constantly moving wheel will carry you to the top if you allow it, or back down if you aren't careful. The 3 characters are reacting differently. The snake is fighting to maintain its position, so it doesn't go down. Fearing to take the short-term difficulty to get back up, the dog man is rests on the wheel, allowing it to dictate his position the entire time while the sphinx (holding a sword, which represents the mind) maintains its position on the top because it is clever and realizes what works. The four characters in the corners can represent the zodiac groupings of Air, Fire, Water and Earth (also the 4 suits). They are learning and watching events unfold.

This is a great card to appear anywhere in a reading. It shows that the position is changing for the querent for the better in that area. A major shift in how they experience life is certain, but they need to maintain that position. This can be a card about learning what works, what is welcome and feeding that source. The wheel keeps turning and if they lose focus or rest on their laurels they will soon be back down to a hard position. I often find that this card can help someone really analyze their situation and decide what would be a good position, helping them realize how to avoid slipping back down to where they came from. Much like the Sun described later, this is a card that draws huge relief with the idea that things will potentially be improving.

I put myself in an extreme situation, so I had no choice but to climb back. I was homeless, jobless and there was a minus symbol before the three digits of my bank account. But I felt fine, I knew I had been to the bottom of the wheel before when it was forced on me and if the worst came to worst. I was prepared for it, I was literally ready to die, not inviting or encouraging it. But there was no fear of it.

This time, however, I dropped my position so I could let myself get back up on my own terms. I sold off all I could, got rid of many things I had no need for, put everything else into storage and loaded my car with all my holistic equipment, a bag of clothes and a £35 16-year-old single man tent and went on tour.

I had no purpose other than to see where I ended up and clear my head. I travelled across Scotland and England meeting up with people I had met at fayres and doing readings in pubs and cafes to pay my way. I was spreading out and connecting with people that would have otherwise been unaware of my existence.

Nightly I would find somewhere secluded but close to a local swimming pool with shower facilities to set up camp and somehow, I wasn't panicking. It was f*cking hard. I am not a small man and I found it so uncomfortable in the small tent and tight sleeping bag.

Not to mention we were heading into October, so the weather wasn't very forgiving. Some nights I would take payment in drinks so I could get drunk and sleep in the car a little easier. Again, I am not built for sleeping in a car, so this was the only thing that helped.

To my surprise, people were interested in what I did and during this period of sleeping rough, showering at local pools, and using laundry services where I could, I met some really amazing people who gave me a broader insight into this thing we call life.

At this time, I felt truly isolated from everyone. I know I didn't help myself and I am certainly not trying to paint myself as a victim, I always hold myself accountable and I know I hurt people during my period of mental depravity. Something that surprised me though was the olive branch of my old journeyman, Sebastian. He lived in England with his wife Samantha (who wasn't keeping good health). He was a Geordie (Newcastle area) and he was always full of lessons. In fact I still practice some of what he taught me. One of his most important and useful lesson was how to make it look like I am busy when I am actually doing f*ck all. They took me in for a couple of days and although I hadn't worked with him in many years, I still learned something from him.

He always lived very frugally, saving up for their retirement. But things didn't work out how they imagined so he basically wasted a lot of his life, scrimping and saving and missing out on so many wonderful things. He expressed some of these regrets to me. There were a few other wine-induced chats which really reinforced why I had to do things for myself and not stress too much for the future if I was to get to 75 and have a regret-free existence.

Less than 48 hours later I met another 75-year-old who had the opposite philosophy to Sebastian. I was walking up to a castle in a place called Tarbert and he struck up a conversation with me. It was very interesting to have met someone in a very similar position to Sebastian with a different outlook, he spent all his money and had no regrets. It was like I was deciding between heads and tails. They were opposite sides of the same coin, giving me both arguments before deciding my stance. It was truly a destined encounter. Things felt like they were about to take a lovely turn for me.

Unexpectedly I received an invitation to the biggest holistic fayre in Scotland, at the 02 in Edinburgh. It was a real shot at launching myself to a fresh audience and I didn't want to waste the opportunity.

Another morning I was having breakfast while waiting for my washing to get laundered and I received a phone call from the workplace I left asking me back. I refused initially but they offered me a flexible position to fit in with whatever I wanted to do; it was week to week. It sounded great, no pressures as I was classed as a third party, some extra funds and security while I could develop myself in a more controlled manner.

The same afternoon my landlord asked if I knew anyone who was looking for my old flat because the tenants who took over from me had to return to their home country unexpectedly. After explaining my situation, he agreed to let me back in.

Again, it seemed like the universe was rewarding me for taking such a huge gamble. I had some serious takeaway lessons from this point in my life, along with the realization that I really do not like camping. It looks great in the adverts when people are gathered around a fire with a guitar, some marshmallows a badminton set and smiles all round, but fast forward to the morning after and show the reality and it would put folk off. (I understand some people do like camping, that's their problem.) My spine felt like it was in a permanent fetal position for some days after this.

It felt like I kept getting pulled back to Peterhead. Despite my attempts at leaving over the years I couldn't seem to break away and that was something that frustrated me so much.

But I decided to embrace it and not fight it anymore. I obviously had work to do there, in spite of its protests.

Justice – A man sits in a position of authority, holding a sword in one hand and scales in the other. A symbol of the sides of justice, it could be cruel but fair. The crown indicates that justice is on a par, or above that of, royalty. Although a similar energy to the Hierophant, there is only one character. He is not there to guide but to judge after listening to each argument. His feet position is different from the Hierophant as well in that he looks like he is willing to take action.

Fairness, payback, legal activities, or someone not connected but having an impact on the situation, are the most common meanings behind this energy. It is a pretty straightforward card to interpret when it appears and normally the querent has no issues in placing it in their life.

There was a particularly difficult reading for a young man I conducted. It was at his house, and he was very closed off. He made me really work for it, but there were a lot of major arcana in his spread. The combination of Justice and the Star (among others which preceded them) indicated that the ex-lover and *mother of his child would have a huge moment of clarity based on a legal event. He broke down and informed me that he had been threatening to take legal action for a while regarding custody of their child, but he kept pulling back. I suggested that he follow through with the threat and he would notice a change in her. It was a great relief for him. Last I heard the threat worked, they were able to work something out to benefit everyone but that's all I know. It was a very powerful reading. Because it was so slow and basic, these cards in combination blew the sh*t out of the reading and everything aligned perfectly.*

With my unstable situation, I struggled to maintain balance but kept moving forward with determination. I had some reprieve with the contract offer and being back in the flat. But this was only part of the equation. I still needed to develop and generate what I needed to really launch myself. I kept doing what I was doing but with more gusto and grit. My passion and self-belief were still there. I knew I had something to offer, and I was dammed if I didn't do everything I could to put it out there.

Most weekends I would travel around Scotland to different events and thankfully I got some regular bookings, but I was still a long way off. Financially I was ruined, barely making ends meet and living by eating food out of jars, yet despite this my hopes were high. I had all but given up on Peterhead but something kept pulling me back. My children were a big influence on this, but it was something else too. For one reason or another I was being kept away from them, so they weren't the driving factor.

I felt there was something higher at work and I needed to figure out what it was. Spiritually I was struggling and this I think was one of my blockages. I had busied myself so much that I didn't have any time to process things around me and that itself was a distraction. I was addicted to the energy of the fayres and doing the readings. I was avoiding life by hiding behind my goals.

Life hadn't been fair to me, but I kept looking at it from my own point of view. I was alone and had been disappointed with those around me because they couldn't give me what I wanted. I had separated myself so much from my family and what few friends I had left that I really felt that this was all I could ever achieve. I started to doubt myself. This was a hard point because I was questioning everything I was doing. I had little faith in anyone anymore and I started to sour in my readings. Many people had a situation I would have killed for, and they weren't happy. I felt a bitterness coming forward.

I allowed myself to get sucked back into the toxic and damaging world of online dating. All I wanted was someone to hold me and tell me it was ok, and I was doing the right thing, and I didn't care who it was. I honestly think I saw the worst in humanity there, and I worked as a bouncer for a time in my younger days. I took every rejection personally once again and I couldn't understand why I wasn't getting a chance because I was offering everything they asked for. It was a very confusing and mildly traumatic experience for me. Needless to say, I removed myself from the world of online dating rather rapidly.

My mental state, although not at the low point it had been in the past, was not great. There were still several traumas I had to deal with, and I was avoiding them by busying myself as a distraction, I realized that I still hadn't properly grieved the loss of my family. Was I headed for another crash? There were a few people I had connected with, but again, I kept them at a distance to protect myself. But I could feel myself shutting down emotionally, I had been hurt so many times before I couldn't bear any more heartache. I was focusing so much on healing others I neglected the most important person in my life. ME. As I will describe later, there were several triggering events during some readings which really impacted me and pushed me to examine myself at a depth never reached before.

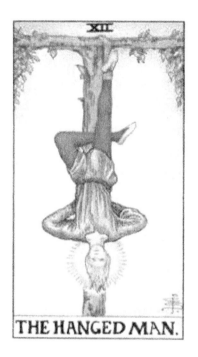

THE HANGED MAN.

The Hanged Man – A man after being judged is put in a difficult position, however it is not hopeless. He examines his surroundings and situation from a new angle and can see how he can move forward with more fortune and opportunity. His upside-down position is similar to how Saint Peter got crucified, but he has more freedom of movement. The halo around his head indicates he is an enlightened person, perhaps by the judgement of his crimes. He has seen a new way forward with better results.

If something feels stuck, not to the point of turning back but where the progress has slowed, the hanged man points towards changing perspective - potentially by putting themselves in an uncomfortable position to do so. Once this has been done, they will see the actions required to keep moving forward. Again, this is quite a straightforward energy. If the querent can't change how they look at or do something they will always yield the same results, and this is often not a welcome outcome.

This is generally another straightforward card and whether it appears early or late in the reading it can change the meaning behind the reading in a way that nobody can predict.

I returned to the spiritual church. I had stopped going for some time, but when I rejoined at the fresh term, I felt like I had returned home. They were all so happy to see me back and there were new faces, new growth, and a new start.

As mentioned, I had tried relationships to no success. There was always something missing and despite my best efforts and pleas they hurt me each time. I had started to grow disdain towards women as I took their rejections personally. I had grown up around women and listened to everything they complained about. At the fayres, markets, and bookings with clients. Often, I would be involved in a conversation or therapy release where they dumped everything they hated about their partner and how they wished they would do things differently. As when I was younger, listening to my mum and her friends do the same, I took all this on board and made the conscious effort to prove to any potential partners that I was not like other men. I would always put a lot of effort into my profile and read others carefully to see if there would be a potential for a connection.

I felt like I understood women in a way most other man couldn't. I wanted to care for them, respect them and more importantly LOVE them. I wanted to show them that romance wasn't dead and if they gave me a chance, I would let them see that they were still of value and could trust again. My dreams of a relationship were very old fashioned (not in a misogynist way) and I quickly realized that it was not welcome in the dating market. I was a friendzone kind of guy and I couldn't change that, despite my best efforts.

During the months prior I had also been getting friendly with an amazing woman who shared a special connection with me. We both felt it. She would occasionally attend my sound baths and had come to me for readings, so I was very conflicted when feelings started to develop. She was involved in quite similar work to me but from a different approach.

After spending more time together to get to know each other but not dating, I decided to take charge and see where it went. We enjoyed each other's company and had great conversations. She felt the same and I knew it. It was the first time I think I ever knew it, her energy changed when I was there, and her eyes told the whole story. I took a chance once more and made my move.

We had several coffees (again, not dates) at the flat but she was afraid of being seen publicly in Peterhead (there is that fear of scandal again in the town). So I asked her around for lunch. I was so nervous the whole day, it was the first time I had felt like that in years. Although I had previous relationships this was the first time since my marriage deteriorated that I felt like I had a real chance with someone that wasn't from a place of desperation.

While I waited for her to arrive, I looked out the window and tried to convince myself that she wouldn't stand me up. She was late. I panicked and my heart sank. She messaged saying she was only a few minutes away. I flustered, lit some incense, and set the table. We had a great lunch. I put a lot of effort into it, I cleaned the dishes, made the coffee and we talked.

With my mind the way it has been conditioned, I try to imagine every possible scenario so I can always react appropriately. I had been preparing a mental script about what I would say. My heart is pounding as I recall the emotions felt. Just as she got her coat on to leave, I asked her to sit down, and I offered my heart on a plate. I explained my feelings, how I knew she felt the same and what I could offer. I expressed my understanding of her situation and my willingness to be patient. This was only the second time I had poured my soul out for someone like that. (The first was with my ex-wife to try and sort out our marriage.) And, like the first time (unsurprisingly to me) it was rejected. She laughed in my face and left with a grin while I stood there sweating and looking and feeling like a right d*ck.

I spiraled once more for a short time, and I decided that love was only a fantasy after all. I was an old soul in a new world and love was an idea of a bygone era. People were too busy for it these days, so why was I so concerned with it. I was fully preparing for another "dark night of the soul" and I wrapped myself in my youngest daughter's quilt and cuddled into my eldest girl's pillow laying on the floor watching romance movies (a self-torture I inflicted on myself each weekend. I prayed to have the kind of experiences they put on screen.) I allowed myself to be convinced that I deserved to be alone, and I grieved; this was the final let go of many things for me. The loss of friends, the loss of dreams, the loss of love. If I was to recover, I needed to accept the fact that my life was destined to be solitary.

I was broken once more. However, something changed. I changed how I viewed the rejection. As I mentioned, I had looked at everything from my point of view. I changed the focus of my loneliness and frustrations about the world and as soon as I did this something clicked.

Death - A skeletal rider arrives to collect the deceased; he carries a flag but no weapon. The horse is calm and under control while onlookers take differing reactions to the unexpected event. A sunset is seen in the background between 2 pillars while boats carry on with their voyage unaffected by the event surrounding the death.

The Death card is the most feared of all, partly because people view it as the end of the line. If Death was the end, it would be the last card. This is also one of the busiest cards in terms of meanings and interpretations, it signifies a great change in the querent's life. How they view that change will affect the overall outcome of their life. If they welcome it, they will succeed; if they don't face it, they will fail; if they don't understand it, they may have some delays; if they try to influence something they cannot control they could end up in a far worse situation because of it. With each change there is a choice to be made.

Once I was doing a small UK tour to promote Tarot and increase awareness of holistic therapies. I was in a bar at Bellshill near Glasgow the night before the holistic Fayre in the O2 in

Edinburgh. I had just finished eating and was sitting at the bar chatting to the locals and messing around with my cards, a few comments were made about Tarot and how it was scary. The Death card was mentioned so I pulled it out (the Death card I mean) and began to explain the psychology of it. I asked a few people around to look at the card for 2 seconds and remember something. This is one card that the more you look, the more you see. A few of them focused on the horse so I asked them what they thought of when they saw it. An older gentleman said racing. So, I suggested games and fun and he agreed. I offered that he was feeling extremely bored and looking for something to excite him, he laughed and agreed because he had recently retired and was spending a lot of time sitting with nothing to do. A woman then mentioned the reigns. I said she was looking for someone to take control of her. (With a devilish spatter of inuendo on my part.) She roared laughing and yelled out in a thick Glasgow accent about how she needed a man to get her pumped. Anyway, by the time I got through this the whole bar of around 20 people, all the staff and some of the kitchen crew, were around me listening with great interest. After a while the owner came down roaring at them all to get back to work, but when he saw what I was doing he listened as well for around 10 minutes. He then gave me some drinks to shut me up so his customers could get served and let his staff return to work. It was a beautiful and surreal experience for me to have such a random audience from nothing.

It was 0200 in the morning, and I had barely slept 6 hours since the rejection a couple of days prior. I was laying there wide awake. But something was different. I was going through not only that event but many others.

I looked at them objectively and not emotionally (easier said than done). For each instance a separation had to be made from me and the event, which was a bizarre feeling, almost like I was bearing witness to something from the outside. Like a slideshow of my life but from the view of a lens instead of first person. It was a rather calming and yet exhilarating experience as I felt I had finally been able to awaken something I had been poking at for such a long time. Of course, I thought I had done that quite successfully since starting my journey but here I was, faced with a familiar situation and having a similar reaction, though admittedly not so severe.

Something common among people who experience trauma is that they develop some means of protection for later life. I discovered what mine was during this event.

One thing I do when speaking to anyone is give them 100% of my attention so I don't miss anything. Little things that may escape the notice of most people, I pick up and think about, I hang onto words and try to see the meaning behind them. I believe this is to help me read someone's intention while they interact with me. Many times, I have been sucker punched or otherwise taken advantage of because I missed something in the interactions leading up to it – like if a bully pretended to be nice to me to catch me off guard or if a female would ask if I would be interested in going on a date before ridiculing me in front of the class when I eagerly said yes. This is the kind of thing I now subconsciously filter. Combine this with me being able to read energy to a point and I feel that now I have a reasonable grasp of people.

I played through all these little things in my head and made some dramatic realizations. It wasn't me who was being rejected. It was the situation, they rejected themselves from the situation because of their own limitations. It didn't matter how ready I felt I was, if they weren't ready it wasn't going to work. This cast my mind back to the woman who I had a relationship with previously who let me down. She was looking for a relationship despite not being able to accept it. My energy was the same. I was looking for someone just so I wasn't alone, it was something I felt I had to have but I really should have examined the energy around it.

The rejection from this new special connection had absolutely nothing to do with me. I just so happened to be the one in front of her. It was insane, all these things started to slot into place and clear instantly, it was like a game of Tetris where the stack is almost to the ceiling when the perfect block drops and the game takes a more exiting turn, and the lines get cleared three or four at a time. I had found something; it was like a spiritual rebirth. I was excited.

I finally understood not only me and my motivations, but those of events in the past. I saw them in a new light and was able to instantly forgive many things because of that. Instead of my heart closing, it opened more. Just not in the way that would have been expected. I loved myself, I understood that I wasn't ready for a relationship either because I had so much work to do.

Temperance – An angel stands pouring one cup into another, one foot placed on the ground precariously while the other is in the water, a delicate position which could easily be affected by the unexpected. There is a dulled halo around their head which could mean that they are not yet fully developed because they are still learning. The sun vanishing in the distance will soon leave the path in darkness and if movement stops, this action of balance will be heavily impacted. This is a very harmonious card which means there is balance starting to appear in the situation, but this is all dependent on the position of the querent. They should pay careful attention to their surroundings and not be rigid. They should take stock and keep moving forward towards the setting sun. This is a big part of the physical and mental composure of a person, the ability to push forward to some more difficult situations. Intuition is building but can be lost if no action is taken.

If I were to suggest something here, it would be that this would be one of the more common Major arcana that appears in my readings.

So, there I was at this point at 0230 in the morning, standing in my back garden in the middle of darkness, gazing up at the glistening stars, clear for all to appreciate and take inspiration from. The constellations, ancient and mysterious, lay spread across the black sky, unaffected by the happenings across the world and were looking down on me as I stood outside in my bare feet leaving voice notes and messages to people like some kind of Halloween Ebenezer Scrooge. It was an overnight change, except (not that I recall anyway) it wasn't several ghosts bringing me warning. I was buzzing, I reached out to the special connection and asked to talk.

She agreed (not at 0230, I'm not that mad) and she listened to me. I had realized some things about myself as well. I wanted a relationship because I thought it was what was missing from my balance, but instead it was the desire for one that was putting me off balance.

We talked for some time and we both were able to clear blockages for each other. (Not in the way you might be thinking.) Who knows, one day it might develop into something more - the phrase "right thing, wrong time," springs to mind. But, for then at least I had to focus myself on my path. I had so much still to do and now I felt like I was finally able to complete what I set out to.

My readings continued and there were a few unusual experiences coming up for me during these that previously could have really derailed me. But this new balance meant that I was able to compose myself in a more controlled manner.

There was an interesting reading with someone which initially I left with an unpleasant feeling, I'll call this lad Simon; when he sat before me nervously, and rather constrained, I picked up quite quickly that he had a hard life and his energy was very unstable. His mother was also in spirit, which he confirmed when asked. She brought a very regretful but loving energy towards him. At the time he was feeling very alone and unloved and was looking for a hopeful outcome from the cards, mostly for a reason to go on. The Tower, The Star, Moon, and Sun card appeared, the outcome was The Ace of Cups and The Ten of Pentacles. He was headed towards an emotional beginning and physical happiness. This had been the only time I had that sequence of major arcana cards. It indicated that he was making steady progress and things would improve for him. He was able to get that hope and honestly it was one of the best readings I think I have ever carried out. The reason I say it wasn't pleasant was because he had dealt with many similar things to myself. During the reading he opened up about abuse that had gone on in his life and how his romantic connections were very one sided and he felt like he was never good enough to be loved by anyone.

It was heartbreaking to listen to, but while he poured his soul out over the cards, I kept relating to what he was feeling and saying. Although I was able to guide and console him to a more positive outlook. I was left pondering my own life and the horrible things I had experienced, and because I was connected to his energy when he left, I had a huge emotional and energy crash for a good few hours.

The reading was one which made me grateful for having had some training as a therapist. This was also a very important lesson for me to be a lot more cautious about my own energy going into readings. As I was going to be doing more intimate readings I understood If everyone had this kind of impact on me it would only be a matter of time before I would not be able to handle doing them. The emotional, mental, and physical impact would build over time and potentially be very damaging to me.

This helped me realize why I was still having energy crashes, especially after doing several consecutive readings. With this and having some major blockages cleared I was finally able to see how unstable my position was and what I could do to change it. I had to take the momentum built and keep moving, I had to stop looking for distractions and trying to balance my life with things which would offset that balance.

The Devil – The Lovers from before, potentially having made the wrong choice, are 'trapped' in a very frightening situation. They are bound in chains and secured to the Devil's perch. The Devil is manipulating these characters into doing his bidding. Blackness surrounds the scene, indicating that there is nothing for them outside of the light that the Devil is providing. But he is using that light to cast a fearsome shadow forward, causing fear and uncertainty for the lovers to release themselves from his control. Upon closer inspection the chains are loose and could quite easily be slipped over the head. The only thing keeping the lovers imprisoned is their own restraint and fear of change.

Addiction, controlling energies and people, manipulation, and ill-intent. Not letting go and trying to control something that is not theirs to control. This is the opposite of the Lovers. It can be an illusion of choice where the choice is made by an unseen force. This can be a very difficult card to talk about because, depending on where the card appears, there is often a very personal and traumatic event which surrounds it. At times it could refer to a third party's involvement. The devil has appeared in many love readings where the relationship is toxic. The chains around the necks of the characters are loose so they are captive of their own accord. This can sometimes have a really empowering effect on someone to hear how bad their situation is and it can cause them to take action.

The Devil has appeared in more than a few of my readings and its impact can be quite severe. It highlights parts of someone's life that they may not ready to deal with at that time. However, as I tell everyone who comes for a reading, I don't control the cards, I just read them. I will not fluff things up and I will be honest and tell you what I see. The way I look at a reading is that the querent has come for a reason, and it is not my right to withhold what I see. Normally when I get to the potential outcome and it's very positive, they understand the need for recognizing their Devil. But it can only be themselves who can let go of it.

They say the first step to beating addiction is to face it and recognize it's there.

That's what I did during this time. I removed myself from as much as I could and re-entered hermit mode. However, this time it was different. It wasn't to plan a direction or to decide on a future outcome, that was already clear. This was something which could directly affect that future if not handled correctly, it was a deep dive into my psyche to discover my blockages, true motivations, and hidden traumas.

A lifetime of hiding who I was and being afraid to step out of line had created so many avenues within my mind it was a difficult path to take. To understand how each trauma affected my current situation and mindset was a wild winding path and not a 2-minute job or something to do while watching TV in the background.

I realized what was controlling me and limiting my growth. My desire to help and heal others was primarily driven by my desire to feel validation and love, the regular job changes driven by a fear of being too attached and always looking for the next thing as soon as I got there.

Ultimately, I wanted to be more than I thought I was, driven by a need to live my own life, but stabbing in the dark for something to stick. I was trying to prove to those who mistreated me over the years that they were wrong, about me, about life and about the future. That was my prime motivation.

My willingness to do more than my fair share of a task and justify my inclusion by helping a situation instead of thinking about it from the other point of view was a way of avoiding my true thoughts and feelings and distracting my mental and emotional balance to a point where if I wasn't 'helping' or working on something I felt lost. I had a deep need to be needed and an enormous want to feel wanted. Hermit mode was temporarily engaged to navigate this stage.

This time hermit mode wasn't driven by circumstances, it was a more conscious effort to return to a previous stage and reshape the path. It was difficult but it wasn't traumatic. The dark nights of the soul were not as severe, and I was finally able to control my emotional output to a point where logic and objectivity were the focus. It was like standing in a library, long abandoned and derelict, empty, silent and with many shelves and sections. Each time I handled was a memory, each chapter contained a lesson.

During meditations and mindfulness techniques I explored each and was finally able to bring the covers together and earn closure for good. It may not have taken shape the way I imagined but it was over. It was a huge relief.

All these things were holding me back. As soon as I let them go things rapidly changed for me. It was like an elastic band was tied round my waist giving me some movement to get so far before getting snapped back into position, getting hurt each time.

But this time, instead of just getting up and walking in a different direction and hoping for a different result, I looked behind me to see what was actually pulling me back.

I ripped that band off as soon as I saw it and instead of having a panicked sprint to escape, I looked around, took a deep breath, and walked like a boss in the direction of my choosing.

The Tower – A violent storm has knocked the crown, which is a symbol of intuition and status. The Tower is collapsing as it was not built effectively, the characters have chosen to leap from the turmoil and escape altogether instead of waiting for the storm to pass and work on improving the structure so it would not be as affected by any future difficulty. The Tower collapsing shows us our weaknesses and reminds us that to maintain a healthy balance we must always be developing and building to enhance our position.

This is the last majorly difficult situation on the path towards completion. The Tower falls because it is not built correctly and cannot withstand external forces. If it is built using the same methods and materials it will fall again. This is like a storm clearing the path, destructive and very difficult. A Tower moment can have major implications in a situation because it will either make or break someone. Will they rebuild, stronger, wiser and with more vigilance? Or will they repeat their mistakes and hope for a better result next time? This energy is about learning lessons and using them to shape the future. A reverse tower can mean that they are building towards repeating the same mistakes.

The tower has made many appearances in my readings, mainly representing a past event that the querent still hasn't dealt with, creating massive delays in them moving forward with their life. If it appears as a current energy, then the querent is still in the energy and the event has happened very recently or will do in the very near future. If the position is as a potential outcome, the querent is likely to be in for a hard time but they can prepare for it and understand that it is happening to clear the path for newer and better things. If you have a basic grasp of Karma you will know that there is a high potential for you to keep repeating things or having similar experiences. This is something that occurs naturally to ensure that you have actually learned your lesson and once you can demonstrate that you have, you are unlikely to have the repeat cycles. You can finally move on to the next thing.

With all the lessons behind me I reshaped my foundation and took the right steps towards my future. My mind was fully aware of what was going on around me and how I felt. When required I would look back just to make sure that I didn't put that elastic band back around my waist.

Something happened while I was doing a series of Reiki, Sound and Tarot bookings at a hotel, for staff and the public. This was something to test my resolve and see if I had learned my lessons. It was a great day with a beautiful setting. They gave me a room at the back of the bar to set up as I wanted and it was a very healing space, especially with the river flowing behind the building that filled the space with a very meditative sound. After I completed the bookings, I sat at the bar to have a few drinks to unwind and think about the days unfolding.

A young woman (let's name her Isobel) approached me and commented about the bear paw tattoo I have behind my left ear.

I explained about spirit animals and guides. She was very interested and after a few minutes of general chat she asked what I was doing in the area. When I mentioned the Tarot, she was very excited as she was looking for someone to do a reading for her.

So, I took her back to the closed-out area I had been using all day as it was very private. As soon as I tapped into her energy, I felt a rush that I didn't expect, it was like being thrown down a water slide. It was shock and adrenaline initially but relief and release when it was over. It was a feeling of passion I hadn't felt in my life. There was something indescribable, we were both shaking and during the whole reading we both felt it.

During the reading there were several points when our eyes locked and we couldn't face each other, the closest reference I had was the reading I did with Veronica, but this was different. It was beyond my understanding and it was such a deep experience.

I can honestly say that I have never had or since had a similar experience to that. It was as if our souls were connected somehow. I was able to maintain my composure during the reading, but her situation was an almost exact echo of my own. At the time I was still quite vulnerable as I had been feeling very lonely and cut off from people. Romantically I had been hurt more often than I would care to admit, and this was the same energy that she was feeding me. We were kindred, after the reading she paid and invited me to have a drink with her and her friends (one of whom saw me earlier for a reading) so as we spoke, the energy remained.

I found it very hard to shut down after this reading, it was more than an automatic or thoughtful action to close our connection. I had to really focus my mind, breathing and thoughts to slow down to a point where I felt I had separated from her energy.

Even though I had energetically closed it was too powerful to ignore. We parted ways and although it embarrassing to admit. I felt like l had felt true love for the first time in my life (barring my children of course). I was infatuated with her. The logical part of me couldn't understand it as we were strangers, and she wasn't (at least in societal norms) so absolutely drop dead gorgeous as to instigate such a response from me. We had spent the whole of around 90 minutes together, but I honestly would have married her at that point were it an option. Before you say, I realize how much of a simp that makes me sound.

I couldn't sleep that night. I kept checking my phone for messages, and she even liked some of my posts, so I prayed for a comment or reason to message her. Even on the drive home the following day she was never far from my thoughts. I gave her a business card the night before and I was praying that she would call me. I had no contact information for her, and it would likely have been thought of as totally creepy behavior for me to get in touch anyway. To this day I have yet to experience a real-life connection that gave me the same chill throughout my being.

As a rule, I hold myself to quite high professional standards. So regardless of my feelings during a reading I cannot let it affect the service I provide.

That was the most pleasant yet confusing experience I can recall ever having during and after any session. But there were still lessons on how to control my energy during reading and it was at that point I asked a serious question. One which could have had serious implications depending on my answer. Why was I doing what I was doing? Was I so desperate for love that I would literally take anything, even remotely positive and twist it into what I wanted to see?

The experience with Isobel was so powerful it really forced me to evaluate where I was at that point in my life. I was using the Tarot to help guide others while giving the kind of inspirational encouragement that Tony Robbins would have been proud of. I could really get people going and more importantly, help them believe that amazing outcomes were possible for them. But while I did this, I was avoiding doing the same for myself.

I felt like I was maybe dealing with my once crippling depression by living a happy full life through the cards and by feeding off the energy and emotions of others. I was clinging on to their hope and happiness with the belief that it would enhance my own life. It was like my Devil; I was addicted to readings and how I felt afterwards. I was feeling lost, dozens of readings in a very short time frame led me to being very drained and burnt out.

Who was I anymore? Was I still me? Or just a vessel filled with the blended energy of many lives? I made the choice to separate myself even further and really explore this new lesson. I stepped back and completed the jobs I had committed to prior, but I needed a break. I needed to rediscover my motivations for doing what I was doing. If it was indeed to escape my own miseries, I had no right to be doing Tarot and advising others on what to do about their blockages when I couldn't do it for myself.

It was another Tower moment in my path, one that would have been the most important of my life to that point. I had dealt with tower moments in the past, but they were mostly surrounding past events. This time, however, was dealing with what was left. Did I build myself up too fast and act before the concrete had hardened, leaving a partially built tower? Was I too focused on getting to the finish line that I had left gaps in my preparation?

Before I could progress, I needed to answer these questions, was my intention still the same? Or was it tainted by everything that had happened until now. After resting myself, these false feelings dissipated, and I examined myself once again with this new experience. This was different however because I understood it was because I couldn't control my energy because of the intensity of the day. It wasn't driven by real emotions. I had simply let my guard down and we kind of gelled our energy together without my realizing it.

This time fortunately, the tower's collapse wasn't so turbulent as previous versions; however, it was the most important because it had a more far-reaching scope in not just my life but for those who trusted me as a guide and mentor.

I have always been a firm believer in practicing what I preach and living by example. If I was able to satisfy the questions, I would continue, with the added mindset of maintaining a more vigilant look on my own life and by pacing myself properly.

I was focused on building the tower back stronger than before. This might seem like a great plan, but it isn't until you build the right foundation that your tower can truly stand up to the world around it. My foundations had been neglected for years in favor of building quickly so I could move on to the next thing.

Others may think that the location doesn't matter, but you could still have a solid foundation in the wrong place. It's the whole event around the tower, foundation, and location, which has an impact on how effective it is. I am the only one who can control all these elements and this lesson was one of the most important ones I feel I have learned. Despite my previous beliefs, it was possible to trust people. But I needed to be considerate about who that trust is presented to. It was my choice who it was and what I gave them. I had been reckless with my time, energy, and heart. Literally giving them to anyone who asked or offering them to anyone. I was so afraid of being lonely I would do anything not to be. I needed boundaries and had to respect them.

This co-operation between myself and the external world was something new to me, but it was something I had to do. I needed to commit to learning but this time it wasn't a physical skill or knowledge. It was far deeper, it was spiritual, it was emotional, it was how to balance myself correctly with not only my environment but those within it. The fool after all doesn't complete his journey alone and if he truly wishes to reach the end, he cannot afford to lose sight of that fact.

Previously I felt like I had no choice but to do it alone and, being realistic, I had done all I could by myself. I needed to change my perception on relationships, expectations, boundaries and respect each element of them. This was going to be the greatest version of the tower I had ever created, because I was building it with the correct attitude for once - carefully, methodically and to a plan.

For the first time I felt my goals were clear as I wasn't purely focused on the end result, I put in place timescales and desired outcomes. I started at the end and worked my way back and built from a point of balance. The environment didn't need to change, I had projected a lot of my doubts and desires onto my external environment and circumstances. But this was not the reality and I needed to change how I reacted to it. This was a grounded position with my whole being. Day-to-day I felt lighter, less stressed, and more present than I ever had before.

I welcomed the challenges once again. It was a statement to life that, if that was the best it could do to me, its best wasn't good enough. I was on form.

Because of how similar and straight forward the following cards are, I will combine them into the same area for simplicity and to save it sounding like I am repeating myself too much.

The Star – The figure resembles the angel from the Temperance card but this time there is no halo. This indicates that the intuition has not developed. The position of the character as she waters the pool and ground at the same time is very limited and unbalanced, the clarity of the star should let her see its time to move on from their fruitless activities. In the background there is a bird who watches and waits for the right time to act, which could mean that patience is required. No further action is required, simply the determination to keep moving towards the end goal.

Once the tower has been rebuilt and is standing up to the external forces which caused disruption, the sky clears and the star appears, bringing with it a moment of clarity and guidance to see the path forward. This is a wonderful energy because until this point the outcome may have been an idea, a fantasy. But the Star shines new light on it and the outlines are starting to be seen, although not complete. The end is in sight, like a lost ship finally catching a glimpse of a shore. This could indicate impatience and the realization of wasted efforts. It is also a sign that it's clear and ok to move forward.

THE MOON.

The Moon – A wolf and a dog howl at the moon, something they can't understand or impact. While they are distracted, a crustacean emerges from the dark waters, an unseen threat which could have a severe effect on the canines if not avoided. The pillars seen in the Death card are now closer and the path between them, although only partially illuminated, remains clear. The moon can represent cycles, secrets, and inner illumination.

Secrets and unseen factors, distractions, and hidden dangers. The path that was shown by the star is not as clear, but the dangers have been left behind (but are still there). This card represents repeated cycles and letting yourself be distracted by things you can't control. This can be a card of warning not to slow down or become docile but to keep moving because to stop now would be to waste everything gained to this point.

I once had a mini one-card reading with a couple and they both pulled the moon. I said that it was like an old married couple arguing but the man was focused on the TV. That was well received as good banter.

THE SUN .

The Sun – A child, naked as the day we are born, sits atop a white horse, happy and accepting. The horse is in control, but the area is walled and safe so no harm can come to the child. The Sun watches and with its warm loving light happiness and fulfilment fill the scene.

Often referred to as the happiest card in the Tarot, the Sun is innocent, letting events unfold with full trust that it will be ok, watching something finally conclude and be genuinely happy with it, moving forward with the finish line clearly in sight. There is no need to be wary of dangers, conflicts, or any other distractions - the Sun is the end of the journey. The sight of the sun is often met with a sigh of relief.

Readings are always flipped into a new dimension with the sun. Often it can be in reverse, and this can indicate that the only thing blocking the happiness of the querent is the querent themselves. They are in their right environment and the conditions are perfect for them, they just need to pull back a little to enhance their perspective and see it.

The thing about having some clarity is that you notice how much time and energy you have wasted on things that you can't affect. Like worrying about how others perceive you. Because I was so worried about that, I prioritized the needs of others while suppressing my own personality. It was such an energy tap; I didn't realize how much of a draining experience it was.

That was something I had been doing my whole life, only letting cracks burst out now and again when I was in different company. It was as if I was embarrassed to show those closest to me who I was for fear of their rejection. My childhood abusers and bullies instilled a massive blockage in me. "I should be grateful for anybody who lets me spend time with them." And this was something I didn't let go of until I began my spiritual path.

All the nervous ticks, intrusive thoughts, illogical assumptions, and emotional reactions. These all made sense, in that I could trace them back to a particular trigger and deal with it. As I removed these triggers going forward the path became clear. Instead of staying and repairing the tower due to poor construction I was able to leave for the first time and continue my path.

I tried so hard to be whoever I had to be in certain situations. I didn't realize I was doing it, and this had a massive impact on my confidence because again I was left with a feeling of regret for not being able to be who others needed me to be. As I started to re-discover myself and work through my blockages and traumas, and as I started to meet people within the community and engage and take on clients, all those self-limiting beliefs faded away into the background until they literally drained out of my system.

I felt like a snake as it sheds it skin. This can represent new beginnings, leaving the old and useless and starting again. Now I had removed the old skin and what was left was 100% who I was, and nobody was going to change that now. But this time it wasn't just words; it was a true belief. A self-belief that was helpful to me and not something that held me back. I was able to stand up and walk forward with conviction, strength, wisdom, experience, and my goal in sight.

With a new mindset, fresh energy pumping throughout my body and with a soul on fire, I was marching onwards like a toy soldier, but one with badass armor and a sick battle-axe (I'm all love and light, honest.) Nothing was going to distract me now, all the little things I let sidetrack me before. Like "what will the neighbors think?" had now become "F*ck the neighbors, they don't do anything for me so why should I care?" Worrying about money all the time and putting pressure on myself to perform literally got left at the side.

There were still some down days of course and moments where I couldn't think straight or see clearly but in general, I was havering less and the drop downs in mood were a lot less common, so I generally felt happier and more positive than before. And thinking about that, I went from about 65%

happy to 85% just by clearing my head, letting my ego step back and allowing my new form to emerge.

Although I could never anticipate all the hidden dangers or future challenges, I felt better prepared to continue forward without being sidetracked. My determination was tempered, and I felt that I was finally able to achieve balance between my mental and emotional parts, the swing of the pendulum not as far spread so the high moods and dramatic crashes were becoming less frequent and more stable over time.

My daily mindfulness was becoming more automatic as I naturally analyzed my feelings and held myself more accountable than I used to. On the days I felt low I knew why and what I could do to elevate myself instead of justifying my misery by blaming it on others. When I felt myself being triggered, I would mentally step back for some scope and understand what it was specifically that was the trigger.

There is a huge feeling of empowerment when you take accountability for your own thoughts, feelings, and actions. This was a different sensation than I was used to. I was accustomed to my energy fluctuating and riding the highs and hiding behind the lows, but this more stable, consistent level of energy was more powerful and controlled. It felt like it was actually unlocking something, like a drunk man trying to locate his key in the lock after another boozy Friday night, his hand swaying back and forth, getting closer each time as he instinctually thrusts the key forward in the hopes of entering his home silently so as not to rouse his sleeping family.

The pace might have slowed to avoid derailing but progress is progress, and one thing I recognized in myself is that my patience wasn't a virtue. I would launch myself into things without thinking, planning, or being prepared for the inevitable failure. But that was replaced with more understanding, self-discipline and of course, patience. This time I was doing something for the right reasons and not as a reaction to something else or to escape whatever situation I was in. I knew how far I had come and how much farther I needed to go, the cycles repeating each time to bring me closer to my destiny.

Now that the end was in sight, I had met all the challenges, conquered my demons, and cleared blockages. It felt like this part of my journey was finally ending. I was happy with how everything had progressed, nothing was rushed. There were no lingering issues to bring forward or knock me back to the beginning and more importantly I was truly content with everything around me. Though I understood that I would need to begin a new cycle eventually, this was a period where I could literally sit back and do nothing more than enjoy the ride.

I felt no pressure or guilt to keep myself busy, I was picking and choosing what I did, and it was the first time I had that kind of freedom of my time. Of course, I was still having to work to pay bills, but the fact that I could say no and take a day to myself was such a welcome reprieve from what I was accustomed to. Although far from being financially independent, I was able to reduce my costs and by realizing how little I needed in my life I was able to make my money last longer.

I was investing in myself; my future and I knew that eventually it would all come full circle and I would be in the position I had visualized.

Environmentally I was in control, the people, places, and influences were all intentional and even those who may not be intentional were instead placed in an appropriate place for my energy expenditure. Of course, there were improvements to be made but compared to where I had come from this was paradise.

My confidence was through the roof, my self-worth was something real and not buckled by my desperate need for love and affection. I was able to step into the right shoes, ones that I picked myself.

Judgement – An Angel plays a trumpet, signaling to all below to rise and be blessed with a second chance. The people below are awakened after a period of rest and welcome the new start, their arms wide, welcoming and open to new possibilities. Clear mountains stand fresh in the background indicating a clean slate.

Although the journey is completed with the Sun, Judgement is the card of rebirth, renewal and second chances. There is no reward in merely completing something, this is the reward. Like the phoenix rising from the ashes, this is letting go of the past and all the pain while retaining the lessons learned and the experience gained.

There is a saying. "The brighter the light, the darker the shadow."

This basically means that by focusing too much on the light, you can miss something important in the shadows. It's a reminder that we need to balance our attention so that when the darkness catches our attention or catches up with us, it is not so traumatic. I understood this at this point.

As I stepped out anew, I felt transformed and although remaining mindful of everything I had to go through to get to this point, I was not letting it define me or distract me. This was a rebirth in its most spiritual sense.

All the previous lessons from not only the preceding cycle, but every cycle that led me to this point were analyzed and learned from, figuring out what I would be willing to do and accept from not only myself, but those around me.

Like the snake who sheds its skin when it doesn't serve it anymore, I did the same, the phoenix bursting out from the ashes of my past with new vigor, revitalized. Nothing, and this time I meant it, NOTHING was going to get in my way. My past had been cleared and I was looking to the future with the patience and determination needed to clear the obstacles instead of avoiding them.

The change was commented on by many people who had seen me at various stages of my journey and that was evidence enough. It wasn't just internally I had changed; it was physically as well. My actions matched my attitude, and I was in sync. Andrew Version 2.0 was finally released with only minor patches required after release day to maintain efficient functionality.

As I walked on with barely a look back, I knew exactly where I had come from. There was no need to look back because the path behind me was clear, and with my new pace and discipline when it came to the path ahead, I wouldn't skip steps, I would take the time to remove any obstructions, so it was clear when I eventually moved forward.

The World – A woman is presented in the center of a wreath, her position like that of the hanged man but her position much stronger, giving her increased scope of vision. She holds a wand in each hand. The red knots top and bottom resemble the infinite loop as seen in the magician and the woman in the strength card. As above, so below. The four characters at each corner represent the suits, the elements, and the zodiac. She is being observed as a master of each.

She has been able to complete her growth and is the true conclusion at last. Mastery of all elements around you, with observers in awe. The Fool has come back to where he began, better, stronger, wiser than he ever thought possible. That leap of faith at the start of the journey took him back to the beginning but with the ability and means to overcome anything.

With a new perspective, looking at past, present and future from a higher place, I felt ready to embody my new spirit, the chaos which led to the tower's collapse now distant and learned from.

My current situation with all the options and avenues for me to venture down was just waiting on that decision and first step to begin a new cycle. The path ahead might be shrouded in clouds but there was a sliver of light piercing them to show me that it was all going to be ok. With my lessons learned and new skills and experience to bring forward, I would not repeat previous cycles. This next cycle was to be a completely fresh start with new challenges and exciting people waiting to help me. This time I would allow them and not avoid things just because they were inconvenient or time consuming.

I was back, I was better, and I was ready.

Not that my path to become a confident healer and Tarot reader has concluded. I am under no illusions that I can claim to be a master or that I have learned everything I can. But for now, at least this cycle has concluded and I am in a position where it's up to me whether I continue to move up the ladder or step back down.

I am back where I started, a mere man with a desire to heal the world one soul at a time, but instead of just having that ideal, I now have something more to back that up.

My journey has been turbulent and full of lessons, but I endeavor to use these to improve myself going forward. Repeating mistakes is not an option because now it's more than just my own life that I am affecting, it is the lives of the millions … and millions (that was a reference to Dwayne 'The Rock' Johnson's promos when he was a wrestler) of people who I will be working with in the future, and they deserve nothing but my best.

Back at the beginning, like the fool. But with a new mindset and skillset, ready to proceed and start anew and prepared to go through the same cycles farther down the road when it is required.

My spiritual work has still got a long way to go and, as I develop, there is no doubt that this will improve all other aspects of my life but, like every journey, it doesn't end. It just opens a new path.

Through evolution and progress, life is unlocked in stages, and this has been a huge stage for me to complete. After years of hard work and a lifetime of blockages to clear, I was ready to take that jump to the next level. The foundations are solid, now on to the next phase of rebuilding my ultimate tower and unlocking my final form.

Fools Journey Concluded

With my journey complete for this cycle and, with my explanation for the cards combined with my own examples as they relate to my journey, I hope you can see how you can relate the major arcana to different stages of your current cycle. The beautiful thing with Tarot is that it never truly ends.

As I mentioned at the beginning, I described the most accepted points with each card on the fool's journey and there are even more points that can be unlocked with further examination and with greater context in a larger reading. In fact, some may even disagree with me on some points, that's one of the wonders of the Tarot, everyone can interpret them as they see fit and add individual depth and flow as it resonates with them.

I trust there's enough information for you to begin to understand some of the implications of each part of the major arcana and that if a reader were to get it wrong or to focus too much on the more general meanings than explore the specifics to make it relevant it could be quite an uninspiring or potentially traumatic experience for the querent.

There have been quite a few people who came to me for a reading for the first time or the first time in a long time because they had a bad experience previously or heard from a friend that it wasn't great.

People still have an expectation of being told bad news and are put off even exploring Tarot out of curiosity.

So as a general point of explanation, the major arcana can be thought of as the inner world of the querent and their thoughts and emotions towards events. Or I suggest that these are big events that will occur in the querents life. It's just a case of when. Depending on the structure of the reading, the position of the major arcana, blockages, and everything else connected to the event.

It could be quite quick or delayed until certain criteria have been met.

Chapter 4:
The Minor Arcana

The Suits

The Minor Arcana is more about the external world and events in the querents life, and it breaks things down into slightly more specific details because there are more cards to interpret. So, if the major cards describe big events, these are smaller events which could relate to the situation and can let the querent understand what they need to work on or change in order to move on with it. The minor arcana is split into 4 suits, each split into 10 pip cards plus 4 court cards. Each suit has a general representation of (as I like to call it) the human condition. These are:

ACE of CUPS.

1. Cups - water energy, fluid movement, social and emotional implications, and romantic relationships.

The delicate balance of our emotions can easily be swayed or spilled over to leave us defeated. The range of emotions during the path of cups can vary from the happiness of exchanging cups with a partner, celebrating with friends and daydreaming about your options to the sadness of letting go of the past, focusing on something you can't change or walking away from a stagnant situation. These basic elements combine with the potential of reverse readings and a card position which alters the emotional meaning behind each. Out of all the suits the cups are the most common that appear in my readings. I find that the querent is normally driven to seek answers because of emotional difficulty or that they are looking for a way to deal with someone close to them.

ACE of PENTACLES

2. Pentacles - earth energy, solid growth, physical aspects of life such as work and non-romantic relationships.

The body we have and actions we take. From trying to navigate a life-work balance, showcasing your abilities and seeing the fruits of your labor, to finding yourself out in the cold and reaping a bountiful harvest. The spin of the coins can be massively helpful or a great hinderance, depending on what you are working towards and your commitment to making it so. The suit of pentacles is what represents solid but sustainable growth. Work is normally the main focus in this suit, but the offers could be of a different sort of physical meaning, depending on the context of the reading - from new business to finding satisfaction in what you are working on. The energy is generally quite slow to act but once they do they have great momentum. All they ask is that you don't fight them.

ACE of SWORDS.

3. Swords - air energy, short lived or lingering inspiration, quick actions, thoughts, ideas, and communications. The logical part of the mind.

The dangerous and often quick actions of a sword's blade can cause some serious pain or cut the ties that bind you to an unseen terror. Choices made blind in a dangerous environment can lead to severe conflict and end with poisonous thoughts holding you down, helpless as night ends and another unwelcome dawn cracks the sky to highlight the stresses that linger from a refusal to address them. However, there are lessons to be learned in defeat, and there is a role for heartbreak in a story and letting a stranger take you to a new shore to start again. The swords are (in my opinion) the most complex of suits because they are involved in the mind, communication, and the opinions of others. They could be described as a trouble suit of cards as there is a lot of conflict in the imagery, but they are merely highlighting issues that need to be addressed before they become mentally and physically damaging.

ACE of WANDS.

4. Wands - fire energy, passion, multi-purpose, general energy towards something like enthusiasm and attitude. Not so much logical or emotional, but physical energy.

The energies causing us to act are a rollercoaster - from making the choice to leave a safe but uninspiring place and walking forward to a new destiny to fighting to maintain a position of strength. The Wands are an exciting but challenging set of cards to complement each part of a cycle. The varied passions of the wands are what motivate us to keep moving and to strive for better. However, the warning is that if we burden ourselves too much with the expectations and energy of others our progress will be slow and unguided and if not handled correctly, eventually the wands can transform into a sword and change how we think of ourselves. If someone was to ask me (I am imagining you will, dear reader) what single card appears most commonly in my readings, I would say the 10 of wands would be a contender for that title. Generally, this card means that someone is being burdened with the energies of others and they blindly take on more than is necessary.

General Meaning of The Numbers

The numbers from 1-10 relate back the major arcana of the corresponding number, so the Aces align with the Magician and the tens with the Wheel of Fortune. This can be used to help with more direct placement of the area. But as a general explanation I always suggest that the 1s (Aces) are the start of something and the 10s are the conclusion. So, for a short example. A 7 of Cups energy is around exploring options which could change the final outcome or halt it altogether if a decision isn't made in due course. A 7 of Swords is about being strategic or watching those around you for deceit, again this could work in your favor or not with regards to the final outcome. These are more easily placed as they are quite specific with their imagery and represented energies.

So, for further context let's imagine the path below in terms of a project.

1 + 2 is the idea and planning stage. (Magician and High Priestess)

3 + 4 is acting on this plan and moving forward. (The Empress and Emperor)

5 + 6 is a hurdle to overcome with some potential conflict. (The Hierophant and Lovers)

7 + 8 is finding the balance once again and re-organizing. (The Chariot and Strength)

9 + 10 are the final touches and completion of the plan. (The Hermit and Wheel of Fortune)

With these ties to a major arcana regardless of whether they make an appearance or not. If you understand this connection, it makes learning the cards far easier as you can understand how it may relate to the querents reading. So even if you only focus on learning the first ten Major cards, you will have a great starting point when doing readings as you would need to work with the images instead of trying to remember anything else.

Specific meanings of the Numbers:

Now that you have a general idea of the numbered cards, we will check out the imagery and build a more focused idea of what they could mean for a querent in a reading.

The Aces represent a new beginning, so this indicates that the querent is going into something with no external burdens. If they have come from a difficult situation it can mean that they have finally let things go and are focusing on what's important to them. If an Ace is in reverse it could mean that they are unsure of what they are looking for.

The Cup represents the heart, and the image shows an overflowing of emotions, the querent is letting go of what they don't need, and the dove represents peace and serenity. They are finally getting rid of the stagnant water and replacing it with exactly what they want. This could be a new relationship, a fresh start with a current lover or a new friend coming forward. Regardless of the exact situation, they are going to be very happy with it.

ACE of PENTACLES

The Pentacle being a physical thing can mean that a new vocation is looming. Whether it is a new job, change in financial situation or a new hobby or pastime. This is something that indicates the querent is beginning a new path and it will require some work but its something in line with their goals. The garden path suggests they are leaving something established but heading towards new pastures to start again because there is nothing more they can do in the current situation.

The Sword representing the mind means that a new idea or mindset is developing. How the querent communicates with their environment and what they think will change in a massively positive way. The Crown indicates that their intuition is true to their thoughts and there is an alignment between the mind and spirit. Clarity and focus will follow with this card.

ACE of WANDS.

Wands meaning passion and energy, something that is starting will fill the querent with excitement, passion and enthusiasm to get going. This might be a short-term thing however if the other emotions, thoughts and actions don't catch up with the initial burst of movement. I would explain this as an explosion of energy, once the movement has started you will need to keep the momentum going. There is a castle in the distance, so if the querent is nearing the end goal they may have a sudden adrenaline rush to complete the journey faster. But again, we need to be mindful that we are not losing control.

The Twos often represent a choice. But also, that there needs to be a balance established before the querent can move forward.

In terms of a relationship, there needs to be equal give and take. This is a balanced exchange, and both are happy. The male being a little more forward than the female here could suggest that one is pushing the other more and is instigating the partnership. The animal emblem can mean a third part witnessing the event to ensure fairness or that the querent needs to make sure everything is how they expect before committing to it.

This character is struggling to balance the two pentacles, the loop meaning that this is unlikely to change anytime soon. There is turbulence in the background that the character cannot see or react to. I often refer to this as life-work balance. The position of the feet can mean that time is critical because this balance is not going to last forever. A choice has to be made on what to focus on and allow the situation to settle before taking on any other responsibilities.

The woman with a blind fold on and holding up two swords. Only one of them is her own. The position is not comfortable, and the cold of the night leaves her feeling that it is worse than it is. She needs to decide which sword to lay down so she can remove the blind fold and walk to a more suitable position. This can be conflicting ideas or allowing others to influence her thoughts. Either way, it is her who is remaining static.

A man stood within the boundaries of his safe space, he gazes out at the world and realizes that there is more available than what he has experienced. Although he is comfortable and safe, he feels an urge to leave. One wand is fixed and does not need support, but the other is his own. Again, the choice here is whether to take the risk or to remain where it is familiar.

The Threes are movement, the choice has been made and progress is happening. Not to say that it is easy but it is still early so overall the energy is positive.

This is a happy gathering, there could be a party or celebration coming up. This is people coming together under a common theme, they each have something different to bring to the group which is represented by the different vegetables and flowers at each of the women's feet. If we are talking about a specific person in a reading this could mean that there is something significant about a gathering. Like if they met at a party or there could be something to pay attention to with their actions at an event.

These characters are looking for something new, this could be a card about standing out, showing off what you can offer and telling the world that you are confident in your potential. Generally, I would suggest that the querent don't be afraid to put themselves out there in competition. So, whatever it is they are doing whether it is interviewing for a new job or going for a promotion. Play to their strengths and recognize that there is still room to grow.

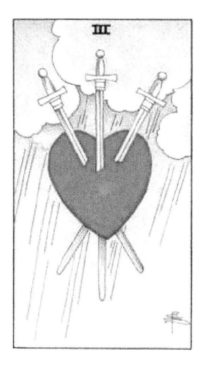

This is a card of betrayal and heartbreak. It could be a third-party situation or that they have been let down multiple times. If these swords are not removed from their heart, it will cripple them going forward. It can mean that the thought of previous heartbreak is affecting their choice to proceed with something, they need to stop thinking emotionally and start thinking logically. It could mean they need to re-examine the past or current situation from a different mindset so they can move on without emotional hinderance.

Now the choice was made to leave the comfort zone, the character here stands with potential options. Several boats could take him somewhere new and exciting, but he needs to decide when to move and which one to board. Time is of the essence with this card. It could mean leaving more behind but all you require is with you. He is clothed in sewn together garments but they serve a purpose, so he has decided to start again. This could mean that the initial surge in energy is slowing down but they need to keep fanning the fires of passion. Like a steam train, if the fires burn out the train will stop.

The Fours are potentially a blockage, now there has been progress with the journey. Confidence can be a factor preventing forward movement. Fear of reverting to a previous situation can lead to stubborn energy.

The man daydreaming under a tree. Potentially wishing for a fourth cup but not seeing that it is being presented to him from an external source. Or he could be wishing for more than he realistically needs or recalling a loss of some kind. Either way, he is stuck in his thoughts due to being unrealistic and the emotional aspect of the card is one of lack or disappointment. Maybe the outcome is not what was expected. He needs to change this focus so he can keep moving forward and not stop just because things are getting hard.

This stubborn looking chap is sitting on the outside of a growing city, full of new opportunities. Unable to move due to holding on to what he has. He has made some progress but is scared to doing anything more for fear of losing what he has. All the while the world grows around him. He could potentially miss out on new opportunities as he has stopped growing his assets. Its time to let go and take the risk.

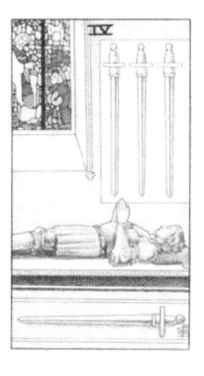

After dealing with the heartbreak, now is time for some quiet reflection. This image is based on an old Knights tradition of having a casket made for them before going to battle. If they returned in a non-living state, they have something to be buried in, if they were fortunate enough to actually return alive, they would lay in the casket and think about the battle and learn from their experiences. This means the querent should take a step back and control their thoughts so they can see that they are still going towards the right thing. It's a temporary situation that should not be lingered in.

This is a small celebration; the two characters could be celebrating a union, or it could mean there is a marriage of some kind. (not necessarily a wedding but a marriage of ideals). More likely if you notice the two characters are moving away from the crowd in the background, it means that they are making steady progress to stand out and are moving towards what they want and are not affected by the actions of others. This can indicate that the querent needs to be focused on smaller goals to reach the bigger one. If we let ourselves get overwhelmed by the whole, we can lose our enthusiasm, but by breaking it down. It is more manageable.

The Fives are normally a difficult energy because it could mean that all progress has been lost if not handled correctly. This is potentially the most difficult part of the journey, like climbing a hill, we are nearing the peak but losing momentum. Extra effort must be made to reach the summit before things start to get easier and the goal is in sight.

This individual is so focused on the spilled cups that they are unable to see what they have left. This focus on loss and the past is preventing them from seeing what they have left and seeing that it's not the end. Lessons need to be learned about why the cups got knocked over and what can be done to stop the situation repeating. The river can be seen as the constant passage of time, again leaning into the idea that the longer they are held in place by the emotional attachment the worse the situation may get.

There are two determined people out in the cold, having come so far despite how difficult it obviously has been for them. A refuge is available where they could stop and recover. There are a few things which could stand out with this. Help is available so if it doesn't detract from your goal, use it. Secondly it could be a message not to stop for temporary comfort because it could stall progress for an unknown amount of time, instead keep pushing forward because the winter is long. Thirdly it could be a reminder that times can be tough and not to let that be a reason not to try. Finally, it reminds you that you are not alone. These people are pushing towards a common goal, and they will keep going until they can rest at the end.

This card is potentially a major conflict. There are lessons learned after every glorious victory and crushing defeat. So, for those victorious, they reap the rewards. But will they reflect and improve for the next time, or will they allow themselves to believe they will always get the same results? Those who are left to return with nothing to show for their efforts, will they develop their skills so the result will be different? The caution behind this card is that both sides need to reflect on what went well, what didn't and how to improve the next time. The defeated can return later and achieve what they want, and the victor can maintain their position on the top by constantly pushing themselves and not stopping.

This card is potentially a minor conflict or training. Even if it's just training, the energy should be the same as if it were the real thing. This card is about maintaining the same level of passion whether it is a minor or major hurdle. These younger characters are practicing their skills with the same intensity as if their lives depended on it. The better prepared you can be when there is nothing at stake, the more likely you will be to walk away unscathed when it counts.

The Sixes are over the bump and momentum will pick up. The worst is truly behind you but there are still things to remain vigilant of.

This is a wonderful card because it can signify children may be involved. But normally it means that teamwork and sharing is encouraged at this point. If the querent is trying to do everything on their own, they will not be able to work to their maximum potential. It also indicates that they should try and have more fun in what they are doing because the worst is behind them.

One must be cautious with their resources. The scales represent balance, the warning being that the querent can be either the one giving or receiving aid. If they find that they are constantly giving, it won't take long before they require something back. Who are they giving aid to? Will they return the same level of support if the roles were reversed? This is a warning to check who is around them and where their precious resources are allocated. Discipline is required if they want to keep enjoying their level of success or if they are in a difficult situation, to seek help but to ensure that it comes with fair and balanced terms.

Are you leaping from the frying pan into the fire? Who is controlling your thoughts? The male is steering the boat, this could be the querent, hinting that there are others depending on their success/ The woman and child don't look happy however, this could mean that they are leaving a hard situation, or they are not happy with where they are going or who is taking them there. This reminds us to be aware of our own thoughts going forward. Are they still our own or have they been hijacked by others?

After some event, people will be celebrating the querent. They may not like this attention, but it means they have achieved something noteworthy. They are head and tail above all others and will quickly separate themselves from the pack. There still needs to be focus so that they don't celebrate too long. They can relax and enjoy the moment as they have earned it. But not to overindulge in this. Especially if they don't want it to be a flash in the pan, keep going because it isn't quite the end yet.

The Sevens can represent that a re-evaluation may be required. Now that you are starting to see the end, it could be a time to start tidying things up and making sure that all around you is what you need and not superfluous. Potentially this could alter the path but not necessarily change the outcome.

The character is paralyzed into inaction because they are overwhelmed with options. Not all will be revealed for each, and a choice must be made. This is time critical as some options may be removed before a selection has been made. There may be more emotional attachments with some options, and this could mean that they need to control their emotions to make the best decision for them.

After working so hard, and some growth has started to happen it can illuminate the excesses around the querent that is not needed. Like weeding a garden, if not tended properly these can impact growth and is very inefficient. The removal of what is not required will allow what is important to grow with no restrictions and will make it more manageable in the future.

This is a card of strategy, thinking outside the box for upcoming challenges. The army approaches in the distance and the thief has taken their weapons. Leaving them ill prepared for any additional skirmishes and they can lose the war because of this. Alternatively, it could mean that the querent needs to watch those around them for deceit or to take back what is theirs, for example if the transaction was not completed honestly and the other party has not fulfilled their duties as promised. This could potentially leave the other party at a disadvantage but being objective and logical, the querent will not let emotions allow them to be taken advantage of.

This person is continuing to engage in conflict despite their advantageous position. They can turn their back and quickly change the situation. Thus, saving their precious energy. This reminds the querent to take stock of where their energy is allocated and that they are still working towards their own goals. Or are they engaging in external events that they cannot affect. The longer this situation goes on the worse the querent will be in the future. It is a card of inefficient use of their energy.

The Eights can potentially represent the final difficulty encountered in the journey, not to lose hope and understand that the end is within reach.

This solemn individual has taken that hard choice to walk away from situations or people that has no value in their life. There is nothing else they can do to affect the cups and it's time to remove their attachment to them. They walk towards the moon, unsure of exactly what is before them, but eventually the night will end, and the sun will illuminate their way. They can see far enough to avoid future conflicts and they understand that there is no time like the present to do this. They can make excuses about waiting for the perfect moment, but this may change how they view the cups.

After spending so much time developing a skill and being consistent with the application of work. The querent has finally got to a point where it no longer feels like hard work. They can repeat results and are happy with what they are doing. They are also working in an environment that is suitable for their needs but not so far away from help or extra resources should they need it.

Like the two of swords, this situation may feel worse than it actually is. Her feet are cold and wet, she is bound and blindfolded. But the ropes are loose and easily removed as is the blindfold. She is making the ongoing choice to remain in this situation. She is not that far from safety and there is still light to help her find her way back. This reminds the querent not to overthink a difficult situation, instead to free their mind and recognize the situation fully and act appropriately.

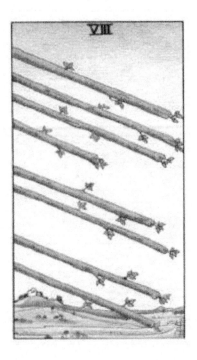

The character from the 7 of wands has turned his back on the distractions and is quickly changing his situation. There are fast changes coming, like the burst of adrenaline upon seeing the finish line. But maintaining balance and control during such rapid movements is important so as not to get overwhelmed and fail so close to the finish.

The Nines are basically the end of the journey, but not quite. This is a point where the smaller things are finalized before the completion. Reflecting on what went well, what could be improved and is the outcome what was initially envisioned.

A man fully in control of his emotions, perfectly willing to share his heart with those who can convince him it's a worthwhile reason. The reckless use of his emotions, which had potentially derailed his progress has stopped and he has taken stock and is protecting his heart with more diligence. This can mean that the querent needs to pull back from a situation and let the other parties do some of the work. They have earned their rest.

Similarly, to the 9 of cups, this card shows a woman who has grown exactly the kind of garden she wants, she has more than she needs and is willing to share, but the lessons from the 6 of pentacles mean that there needs to be a balance between what she gives and what she receives. This is a great energy because it means that the querent can finally start to enjoy the fruits of their labor and can maintain it going forward.

This is a very anxious card. Thoughts are not in control and could be caused by over-analyzing the situation. Others could be the influence here or it could be that they are not able to prioritize what needs to be done so the mind is jumping from one thing to the next without focus. This potentially affect the sleep of the querent can eventually lead to physical ailments and poor health if not controlled.

The wounded warrior stands with his back to wands which do not belong to him. The progression from the 7 and 8 of wands means his back has been turned and the rapid shift in the energy means that he can take some time to catch his breath. He looks back as if considering continuing engaging, or to finally walk away with the lessons learned. This again can mean that the querent should look at where they have come from and what they should leave behind.

The Tens are the true end of something. But is it what was expected or are there still lessons to be learned from this? It could mean that some steps need to be repeated in order to get the desired result.

This is an extremely happy card, like the sun. The rainbow shows spiritual connections and that the storm has passed. Children play and every character is happy with the situation. Family could be represented here but generally it means that the happily ever after is a real possibility for the querent. They may still not see it however if there are still lingering fears or bad habits.

The physical environment has grown to the point where the querent can finally rest easy and see that all around are benefitting from their hard work. Family, friends, pets. All are represented here. The empire has been built, and it's time to either move on to something else or to continue to grow or maintain what is already there. The choice is there.

Unable to control the mind can leave someone unable to act or even get up. First glance at this card is normally met with horror. Again, the situation looks bad, these swords have been placed there by others, reminding the querent to examine who is around them and where their thoughts are spent. There is hope however as there is a new dawn approaching meaning a fresh start is available. But first they need to remove the swords and allow themselves to stand up and walk towards it.

The burdens of others are weighing down this man, he is carrying more than he needs to and cannot see where he is going. Instead of walking away from the 9 of wands, he decided to bring them along with him. This is counterproductive and if he lets go of what isn't his, he can lift his head and see that he is closer than he realizes to the finish line. This can tell the querent that they need to be more ruthless and let others make their own mistakes. We can't save everyone, and our energy has its limits. The longer we carry these extra burdens the more of a drain they become.

The Court cards

There are 4 court cards in each suit which often refer to people around the querent (sometimes referring to themselves). Following on the above general themes of energy and area of impact I will only address the general energies of each with the understanding that they are bound by the suit characteristics (Cups/Pentacles/Swords/Wands.) There is less imagery with these cards so usually they are quite straightforward to place and to interpret.

- The Pages – quite youthful energies that can refer to a younger (or less mature) person. There is a lot of learning to be done before they querent get results.

PAGE of CUPS.   PAGE of PENTACLES   PAGE of SWORDS.   PAGE of WANDS.

When looking at controlling a new aspect of life whether it's emotional, physical, intellectual, or energetic, we need to learn to do it properly. The Pages are the apprentice energy of a person, learning how to handle things in a controlled manner so we can develop properly. These cards are an indication that action is starting to happen, and it needs nurtured if it is to grow, and not rushed. If the Pages are referring to a personality trait, then it could mean that someone is immature or needs to work on something. Other things could indicate that an offer is coming forward, but it will need to be worked on and developed.

- The Knights – More mature and confident energies, they are not at the point of mastering their craft yet, but they are very reliable and capable energies. They tend to indicate that action will be taking place.

KNIGHT of CUPS.　　KNIGHT of PENTACLES　　KNIGHT of SWORDS.　　KNIGHT of WANDS.

The page has become a knight, very capable of handling the element of their charge. They are action oriented and though they may still require guidance from the Queens, they are more focused and skillful when moving. If a Knight shows up in a reading, it's a clear sign that the querent is moving forward with great progress. However, if they come up in reverse it could indicate that they are moving backwards, this is not always a good sign. As you would expect, with the knights indicating action, someone could come in to help with that aspect of the situation or they will remove something.

- The Queens – Feminine energy, more evolved and refined than the knights (who serve the queens) they are very contented with what they have and are self-assured of their status.

The Queens have a lot of gentle energy, not needing to prove themselves to anyone, they tend not to act but rather sit and dictate to those around them. They direct the knights and expect results. Although they are not masters of their element, the masters ensure they have all they need. I take the Queens are quite relaxed energy but sometimes this relaxed mentality can cause some regression if not monitored.

The Queens could mean that a serious offer is coming forward, something that should not be ignored. Personality wise they can be quite cautious but inviting depending on the overall issue. There has been some good progress made with the querent but there is still a little way to go before they can relax fully.

- The Kings – Masculine energies and masters of their realm and in control of all around them. These energies are a sign of huge developments in that area and an unwavering conviction of their position.

KING of CUPS.   KING of PENTACLES   KING of SWORDS.   KING of WANDS

Kings are the masters, they dictate to those how swear allegiance to them, control their kingdom and nurture growth to satisfy their queens and those dependent on them. Although the Kings are not associated with action, that does not diminish their capability. They are ready to act if required and with great skill and efficiency. If a king and queen of the same suit appear in a reading it can indicate a power couple.

A soul connection that should be explored and encouraged. Personality areas could be that the person is very confident and skillful, they can be relied on in troubled times and are confident in their position. It could also mean that instead of being willing to hand out anything, the kings can control and pull back until they need action. Or they can focus and grow exactly what they want.

If a court card comes out and indicates it's a third party to the reading, this is a point where I would use alternate Tarot decks as clarifiers. I can explore the personality, intentions, and anything else that the querent may ask such as their mental or physical state of being. Some of the most common people to come through (as you can imagine) are children and partners. But colleagues, people from their past and potentially someone they have yet to meet can sometimes make appearances.

However, if they are in the same spread as some major arcana, it could present a warning for the querent not to rest on their laurels. For example, the King of Pentacles can be a pre-requisite to the Emperor, a stubborn energy who gets to the top and stops working, ultimately to the point the empire has suffered. Or the Knight of Cups is a similar image to the Death card. If emotions are allowed to run rampant, they could quite easily result in a transformation, just not a welcome or beneficial one.

Generally speaking, the minor arcana more is subject to movement than with the major. This is something that often the querent can control in terms of when they can move forward. Or if others are involved, they can easily impact on the energy to stall or stop progress. One of my more common spreads for blind reading explores the physical actions and thoughts of the querent and often this minor arcana can indicate the imbalance.

I will build an example reading later to add context to this.

Chapter 5:
<u>Reading</u>

<u>The Readings</u>

One thing that should always be remembered is that the readings are in no way shape or form guaranteed to unfold exactly how they are presented. I say they are for entertainment purposes as a way to protect myself, I never tell anyone what to do and the readings are there to give them something positive to think about and provide an alternate context from where the querent is currently viewing things.

Readings are something which can vary hugely from reader to reader so please don't just assume that what I suggest is standard. Almost anything can be covered during a reading, this is based on what the querent would like covered. Love, work, health, wealth, family, friends, or anything else which may come up during the spread.

I tend to structure my readings in a way that is specific to the querent even if they just want to have a blind reading, which is a reading with no specific question or area behind it, and whatever comes up we build from there. Blind reading is often easier because the cards highlight exactly what the querent needs to know. Often, they can't think of anything so it can be difficult to place cards and situations initially, but once they do it gets easier. Off the back of some early cards the reading can take the shape of a work or love reading, for example depending on where the querent places the situations. I cater to each person. I will, however, explain the basics behind a reading's structure using some examples.

The card position is important as it relates to a subject. For example, the first card could indicate the overall current energy of the querent, the second could be a blockage stopping them moving forward, the third could be a past event leading to the current situation and the fourth could be a potential outcome.

Following this structure, I will build an example reading.

1st card: 7 of Cups, 2nd card: The Chariot, 3rd card: 9 of swords, 4th card: Ace of Pentacles

The 1st card could suggest that someone is exploring their options or daydreaming about the future. If it was in reverse, it could indicate that they feel like they have a lack of options or are spending too long thinking about their options to the point where they don't act.

The 2nd card being a major arcana leans towards a big event in their life. The chariot can be thought of as someone leaving their comfort zone, making decisions, and taking control. The reverse could mean the opposite. They are staying in their comfort zone despite how unhappy they are, and they are allowing someone or something else to control their direction.

The 3rd card is a very anxious card suggesting that they are filling their head with intrusive thoughts and other people's ideas, to the point where they can become mentally and physically affected. The reverse could mean that they are starting to let these thoughts go and are working towards clearing their head.

The 4th card indicates that a new beginning is available to them in terms of the physical aspects of their life, i.e. business relationships, work, finances, or habits. The reverse would mean that something is stopping their new beginning.

As a general practice I explain each card as it is drawn so the querent can place its relevance in their life while giving them the chance to ask further questions or explore further. To summarize the reading, I would go from the beginning and tell it like a story.

"It appears that you are at a point of confusion and exploring your options because you haven't been clear on exactly what you want to do and where you want to go, the blockage is suggesting that you need to take control and head towards your target. The catalyst is that you have been thinking about a lot of past events and ideas or criticisms from others. The potential outcome is a fresh start with work or how you spend your time and make money, but only once you make the choice of what that looks like for you."

Let's build on this to see what actions and thoughts are affecting progress, the bottom card is actions, and the top card is thoughts:

So, the action card is the 4 of Pentacles, which suggests that they have withdrawn and are holding on to what they have. It's a protective reaction made in fear of losing what little progress they have made. The danger is that they won't be able to grow anything or move forward unless they accept the risk and let go of their reservations.

The 5 of Cups is the thoughts card; this is a very regretful energy because they are focused on the past, and because of how difficult this was they can't bear to face the future, unaware of how this lack of focus will affect the future. They need to let go of the emotional thinking which is paralyzing their action and preventing movement.

So, once they recognize this and think logically to focus on the potential future, based off them learning from the past instead of repeating the mistakes of the past, they will finally be able to make the decision and steer the chariot towards the Ace of Pentacles.

Especially in a larger spread, additional cards can be used to further explain a situation to provide more detail. This is up to the reader to decide how to do this. I like to use multiple decks in readings to give different messages. So, for example if the querent wanted clarification on the ace of pentacles and the 2 of Wands appeared, it would indicate that they wanted to move away from their comfort zone, and I would suggest that they were looking to change their job, looking for something to give them more passion and excitement.

Additional cards could be the Page of Pentacles indicating a new career altogether and that learning would be required.

A reading can be a very intimate thing and it's no wonder people are often hesitant to receive one. I have been in some situations where a querent has come to me for a bit of fun at a fayre and left in emotional turmoil because of the blockages and events happening around them. I always give a positive outcome but, depending on what must happen first, often people cannot see it as a possible outcome for them. Especially when it comes to a love reading. More than once I have had a reading lean towards an unhappy relationship and even after all the advice cards and clarifications have come out, the querent cannot make the hard choices necessary and so I unfortunately must confirm that their situation will not change.

Many come for a reading and expect to be met with a soothsayer, someone who will just tell them exactly what they want to hear or that they will be extraordinarily wealthy and in peak physical condition in a very short space of time. I don't see the benefit in that. When it doesn't happen, they feel cheated and let down. One assumption is that time is fluid, and it will happen when it is meant to. However, I work within a short time frame so there is actually something to look forward to that's only a few weeks ahead rather than years. Of course, the querent can speed up or slow down this process depending on how they handle things. But I don't invest in the outcome - it's their journey, not mine. I aim to look at the current situation, the blockages and potential outcome, then advise on how to achieve it. The blockages can be challenging and potentially life altering, but the rewards are worth it.

There was one client in particular who got the same message about her relationship multiple times between four different readers before me. She took it as a good sign that the same messages were being presented. However, when she asked me for a reading and complained that things were not progressing despite the continued reinforcement of previous readings. It was different because I built up more than her previous readings. Basically, she was given a warning each time and she kept ignoring it, she was waiting for something else to happen, but it was dependent on what she did with her situation. I advised her to step back and let him make the moves, it had been her initiative until then and she made it easy for him. She told me later that this had the effect she desired and wished she had been told earlier.

Another thing with readings is that they can be addictive. I have had to turn people down because they haven't waited long enough for the last reading to take effect, even if it wasn't me who did the reading. I always ask and if it is less than a month or before something significant has changed, I am reluctant to engage. If we keep getting the same messages, we are more likely to wait for it to happen rather than make it happen.

As I explain to each querent at the start of each reading, I don't and can't control the cards which appear, and I basically lay out a person's life on a table, take it apart, analyze all relevant aspects and build it back up in a way that makes sense. But if someone is not ready to face these challenges, they can leave feeling drained and defeated. Or if they just wanted to be told everything was going to be ok with no effort on their part (hey, you would be surprised how often I get that) they will leave unimpressed because they didn't get what they expected.

Because I tap into energy during a reading and with my empathic nature, I often feel what the querent is feeling and on more than one occasion, especially when I first started doing readings, we have both broken down in tears because of how powerful it was. (I have since learned to control that aspect of myself. Who wants to go to a Tarot reader who can't compose themselves?)

Having said that, I am not immune to these feelings, but I am able to compose myself until a more appropriate time to release the built-up emotions.

Another thing that can massively impact on a reading is how honest the querent is with the reader. On one occasion I was doing readings for a group of friends and one woman was particularly skeptical. I will call her Shiela. Over the course of her reading the cards kept leading me to conclude that there was a romantic situation in the workplace. It was denied repeatedly but, it kept coming back. Eventually towards the end of the reading I had to tell her that her cards made no sense because she wasn't being honest. This led to her confessing (out of earshot of her friends) that she was having an affair with someone at work. This revelation instantly unlocked the cards, and the rest of the reading went great. She was happy with the answers given and the clarity gained from exploring a few potential outcomes.

It's with these types of readings that you really must work and once it resolves, the energy relief can be immense. It also helps build confidence because your self-doubt can kick in if someone shuts down your interpretations. This is also a great lesson for how to conduct oneself during a reading, some people are not ready to hear certain things so once it's clear that a connection to their life has been made its normally best not to refer to that event and move on to more positive and gentler situations in the spread. Once they can place it there is no need to linger. There are many times during a reading when I do a worked example for the card and as soon as I see the querent has made the connection I move on, I don't ask questions or press for them to confirm. I don't invest in the outcome and the less I know the better. If people tell me things that is completely acceptable but my priority in a reading is making sure the querent leaves with some insight into their situation. If they say yes, I believe them and move on. Also, that some people are more reserved than others means that some readings literally go by with me just speaking and them nodding or shaking their head. Sure, it's not fun for me because there is little engagement but as long as they can relate, that's all that matters.

One fayre I attended, there was a lot of interest in me because there was a great build up to my participation, this was after I started to get better known around the circuit. So, when I was set up there was a line of people the whole night, unfortunately I couldn't get to everyone who waited. But there were two friends who came along because they had wanted the experience for years but never had the opportunity.

The first was a great laugh and it turned out that she had a romantic interest in someone who (according to the cards) had a similar interest in her. There were a few other funny situations described during the reading and although she was quiet, her friend (who sat beside her) confirmed everything. This was a brilliant thing. Until it was her friends turn, as I said previously. I cannot control the cards and if you trust a general blind reading, you are placing trust in the reader. There were a few difficult cards that came out for her around her own relationship, it was hard for her to hear some of the words, but she confirmed everything by nodding silently. All of this was hidden from her friend who was horrified at the revelation. I assured her that there was a positive outcome for her, but we explored some areas and she ended up feeling a huge release and she thanked me for being so honest. It would have been an interesting conversation between the two friends after they left.

Most people who come for a reading don't know what to expect so blind readings are more common (at least in my experience). Often word of mouth clients will make a booking because their friend had a reading and when I ask what they are looking for they normally stare back vacantly. I always explain everything I do at every stage because I normally say a lot of things to the querent. Most people record their reading or at least take notes, however if there is a situation that they specifically ask about they tend to have much better recall because they are open to that issue. Instead of a structured reading with set card positions, sometimes people literally want to ask certain questions. I had one reading I remember that the querent (let's call her Sophie) was especially worried about one of her sons, so I based the reading around specific yes/no questions such as:

- Is he doing well?
- Is there anything that Sophie can do to help?
- Will he reach out for help?
- Should Sophie look for alternatives to support?

Even though the answers may only be yes or no, the reason as to why can be told in the cards so that they receive some comfort and ideas on how to get the answer they want. This style of reading can be quite tricky as often it's an area the querent has invested a lot of energy and thoughts. These are usually quite draining as instead of having just one card to interpret with a situation I have (normally) 3 to tie together to give a clear answer to each question. Depending on the situation I limit it to around 4 questions, so the querent has enough information to work from while still leaving something for them to discover.

The most common areas to appear in a reading are work, money and romance. That is as general as they come and it was after doing Tarot for a good while that I understood, despite how varied everyone who found me was, the issues they were facing were remarkably generic. It's amazing to think that not a single experience is unique to one person, everything that has happened to me has happened to many others. What is unique (in my opinion) is the combination of these experiences and our reactions to them. That's one of the interesting aspects of doing a reading.

People come for readings because they need some assurance or justification for how they are feeling. It's not uncommon for me to tell them exactly what they were already thinking but they take the reading as confirmation that their path is right for them. If that's what it takes for them to act towards a better future, I'm more than happy to tell them that. There are some who base their entire life on the outcome of cards, I know of people who read some cards for themselves each day before they leave their home, like the people who would live around the horoscope from the newspapers. This is a very limiting way to live and is putting too much focus on the cards instead of the person taking ownership of their actions. I try and give enough to start and some other details but there is no doubt that results must come from their desire to achieve it rather than trying to line up with what their cards suggested.

On that note it's important to understand how much influence a Tarot reader can have on a person's life, especially if they are impressionable. So, I am always careful with my words and how to put something across to them. I always remind the querent that I am not telling them what to do and the reading is for entertainment purposes. I have heard stories of people trying to sue a spiritual reader because of the information provided during a reading. The querent in these cases had recorded the reading and that was submitted as evidence. I tell a story to them where they are the main characters, the start has led them to me, the middle is what they are currently dealing with and the end of their story is based on how they react to certain obstructions, not from my telling them about every step from now until completion.

There have been a few clients who have gotten in touch sometime after a reading to inform me that I was wrong. I ask them to remind me what was supposed to happen, and after getting a rundown I ask what they have done to make their outcome possible. More often than not, they haven't made the changes required so of course their outcome is not certain. I do a lot of readings, so I tend not to remember much about them. Once I tune in to spirit, I do the reading, then tune down and the reading escapes my mind. This is a protection mechanism as if I recalled each and every reading, I would likely have dementia because of all the lives blending in my brain.

Anyway, they come back and inform me that the situation didn't take the turns I predicted, but when I asked what they have done, often they have done very little. This is why they didn't get the result I predicted. I always say to people that

234

the outcomes are dependent on many things, most of all themselves acting, otherwise I am only telling them what they want to hear. People can often use the cards as a reason not to act, they put blind faith into a reading and wonder why nothing happens.

There was one woman who got the same message 6, yes 6, times and that was just from me, so only spirit knows how many other times she got told the same thing. She couldn't see why things weren't changing for her. I had to say that I couldn't do any more readings with her because unless she acted the messages wouldn't change. She was upset but I had to hold her accountable.

An Energy Exchange

This is the hardest part of being a (spiritual) Tarot reader: protecting your energy. If not done correctly it can be potentially harmful. I mentioned earlier about protecting my energy during a reading. This is something that I have at times neglected and when I did it highlighted a part of me that I wasn't fully aware of.

Part of what makes my readings unique is that being an empath (when I learned what an empath was, a lot of my character and events in my life began to make more sense) I can tune into what others are feeling quite easily and share that feeling. Another aspect I have put great effort into improving is my ability to communicate, especially if I am explaining something new to someone. Once I understand the message, I can break it down so it can be easily understood. This has been crafted over many years while working as a technical trainer for the energy sector.

So, when I pick up on something energetically, I handle it with great care so that the reading is done in a safe gentle way, and I explain it in a clear concise method so that nothing is left unresolved. Some Tarot readers are quite blunt and could use some sensitivity training.

My confidence is also something which has massively improved through doing readings. I have met so many wonderful people and although the scenarios may be familiar, the smaller details are what makes the readings unique.

To tap into someone's energy there must be consent and a willingness to open up. So, in a way we merge and become one. Because of my mediumship training I often get quite specific messages and emotions during a reading. This can enhance that connection and be a very interesting, beautiful and rewarding experience for not just myself, but for the querent as well. There was one reading I recall where my chest tightened so much my breathing was heavily restricted, a pressure built in my head and my throat dried out and became sore. I panicked initially because it was so sudden, literally as soon as I started to shuffle the cards.

After I was able to calm my mind, I asked the querent if there was someone in spirit who had a painful passing, particularly with the brain and lungs. His mother passed with pneumonia, but she had also had a stroke. She was very forceful with her message about him not being honest and letting others control him that she restricted my throat as a way of putting it across. His relationship was toxic and controlling, his mum and his partner never got on and some of his work colleagues were taking advantage of his gentle nature. She wanted him to finally push himself out of that environment because she didn't want him to have regrets. It was hard for him to hear the message but once I explained it, her spirit backed down and let me carry on the reading with no further issues.

Another thing I need to be vigilant of is that I am not just reading my own cards. When I first started, I didn't understand how to separate myself from the querent and the cards reflected that. They were very relevant to my own situation and the querent couldn't take anything I was putting out. Frustrating as this was, I threw doubt over my ability to do Tarot. However, once I developed my abilities and became more attuned to working with energy this stopped and, over a period of time, my confidence increased as a result, but I never lost sight of my initial experiences, so I wasn't destined to repeat them.

However, there were occasionally times where the querent has some very similar events going on to those in my own life. During these situations I am ultimately clarifying to both myself as well as the querent, although I wouldn't admit that as I wouldn't want them to think I was hijacking their reading. But it can be quite enlightening as whenever I have attempted to read my own cards, they always come up blank. I don't even attempt it now and instead go to others for that.

If you remember some of my experiences during my fools journey. I have had some pleasant and unpleasant experiences during reading in terms of how I felt.

The Ending of a Cycle

Although the Major Arcana is a depiction of a journey from start to finish, our lives contain many iterations of this. Every major event or change is broken down into the major Arcana, so it is by no means a single occurrence. If we get married, divorced, have children, move to a new country, leave full-time employment to return to education… these are all huge life impacting decisions which will follow the same obstacles, just that some are more turbulent than others.

In my opinion, the biggest factor in the major arcana as previously mentioned is the World Card. This is the point when the fool has come full circle and returned from whence he came. He began his journey as a blissfully ignorant character with nothing going for him other than the blind faith to keep stepping. Now he has come back, has he learned all his lessons as encountered during his travels? Or is he none the wiser and destined to fail? The key part of the World (at least in my opinion) is that although it is the last number (21) and it signifies the end of a cycle, the ending could be inserted into any slot.

For example, if the fool cannot overcome the chariot, the outcome is therefore to repeat the cycles before it until he can, the World then occurs, and the Fool starts over. The next attempt may take him all the way to the Death card, leaving him crippled and unable to deal with such major changes in his life and belief system. The World card then occurs, and the Fool starts over. One idea to ponder on could be to link the psychology of the Tarot to past lives and Karma.

Regardless of what you believe, if you are passively aware of Karma, the idea of what goes around comes around is a common thread. What you sow you will reap, in this life or the next, the soul bringing forward the hinderances or perks from a life previously lived but not remembered. The basic premise of the Fool's Journey is that he reaches a point where he is a master of himself. He has become one with all elements of life, death, spiritual and physical. He is in full command of his energy, actions, emotions, and thoughts and can take proper movement towards a clear outcome.

Referring to my own path with regards to reaching the end of a cycle. It was using this chain of thought when I looked back on every triggering event I could recall and searched for the lesson in each instance, as I moved from one (character building) event to the other I had to relive some of the most damaging moments of my life. From school yard bullying, harmful comments and physical attacks to sexual assault.

All these traumatic 'lessons' built my character up until I became an adult. It didn't stop there as I explored the outcomes of these previous abuses. Eating disorders, suicide attempts, drug and alcohol abuse, body dysmorphia and to top it all off, (despite how it would have appeared to others) extremely crippling self confidence and trust issues. I was always suppressing what I wanted to do or say to appease those around me, believing what my abusers would say - that I was lucky for anyone to pity me enough to waste time on and that the only use I had was whatever they decided it was.

I was preaching love and light, but deep down I found it hard to believe that love truly existed in this era of mankind. At least I couldn't find any evidence of it. People nowadays have little time for love, at least in the traditional sense of it. Independence, co-dependence, situational relationships, casual, online, options, virtual relationships, the illusion of choice in a saturated market and an endless list of tasks and work to detract from the time and energy to properly commit to a loving relationship. Where was the space for love to grow and blossom? Was I just an old soul, trapped in a never-ending cycle of life over countless years? Had it taken so long for my soul to develop that I couldn't cope in this new world we have allowed to form around us? Was love nothing more than an idea from a bygone era where people were still reliant on the community and with the attitude of "it takes a village to raise a child"?

I thought I had dealt with many of these areas. During my breakdown and recovery, I opened up to friends and family who were completely unaware how bad it was for me (to mixed responses, but hey it was out there and that's a huge step towards releasing).

Everything was hidden from everyone. When the memories first started to come back in my dreams, meditations, and conscious mind, I first shut it down and denied it happened, but then, after I accepted it I started to forgive not only myself and the events, but the abusers as well. It had to be told to several people who, I imagined, were completely shocked when I first spoke of it. However, their reaction wasn't what

I expected. Much like when I couldn't stop the breakdown, I believe the idea was that once I spoke about it, that was a sign I was on recovery. The ongoing concerns and encouragement to speak more weren't there and if anything, it created more barriers between me and my environment. For a long time, I thought the biggest mistake I made was telling people about my struggles. I was still looking at things from my own point of view at that point.

There was little follow up and no check in, how I viewed it was that my trauma was of such little importance that it didn't even register enough for them to bother making sure I was ok. As mentioned earlier their reaction was also a triggering event which led to topics in some of my videos which really didn't go down well.

How can people support those going through some mental health troubles when they don't know how to react? This trigger was very explosive for me at the time (Bubble bath pill incident) and was the catalyst for my friends to suggest Reiki, so it turned out to be a blessing. I have since forgiven everyone (including myself) for everything that has ever happened in my life, in a way that truly separates myself from my past. I retain no anger, no endless search for answers and clarity, and no expectations from anyone that I couldn't deliver myself. It was quite a liberating experience.

I had so many repressed memories and blackouts from my childhood that I couldn't answer some of the specific details. I believe that those who have experienced trauma of any kind shut things down to protect their own sanity and state of being, and these things surface when we are more able to deal with them.

As my mind map and trauma release developed, looking at my reactions as well as those of others around me, I changed how I viewed things, and this then led to my learning an important factor which massively improved my readings - being able to switch from an instigator to an observer. I was guiding people from my point of view till then, that was why I struggled to control my energy, I was walking slightly in front but just to the side as a way of protecting them. But I needed to be behind them, guiding from a distance and observing things from a higher point of view, I didn't need to be right there with them when it was their journey and not mine. All I had to do was take them where they needed to go and be there when I was required. It was a bit of a step back because it was counter-intuitive for me. But when I did this, there was a shift. It was an ending of a cycle and allowed me to move forward in such a powerful way.

This meant I was able to tap into this energy, match it to the querent. I could relate the emotional and logical thought patterns and explain it much like a journeyman would pass his experience in a way his apprentice could understand. The storytelling improved, how I felt before, during and after reading was a lot more focused. Although I did still experience energy burnout occasionally, it wasn't as extreme as it had been previously. I started to trust myself a lot more and that I was doing it for the right reasons, yes, I was (and am) still learning but this is from a point of view where I'm constantly looking to better myself and the service I provide.

Finally, I was the example I needed to be, I was becoming more mindful and present day to day and minute to minute, and this started to pay off as others could see the growth. Indeed, I still have down days like everyone does, but I don't let these temporary moments dictate my future, my passion for it increased and everything else around me seemed to grow as well. From the outside looking in, I may have been quite stoic and cold, at least until I could observe how the people were. I am very careful about my energy now because I have learned the hard way from divulging effort into people before I understand their intentions. But it was exactly what I needed to do. To tap into different emotions and energies without being affected by them and to give clear readings and instructions to those who saw fit to trust their reading to me.

Each cycle ended and gave me a better podium to launch off into my next one, each getting closer and closer. I hope you understand this in your own path and can see that you are never starting again from nothing, you are starting from experience. You will learn and not repeat mistakes. And once you get to your goal, you can start again. Nothing can take away what you have built up in yourself. Unless you allow it.

Conclusion and Final Thoughts

If you have been able to make it this far into my work, you have my thanks. If nothing else, I hope that you have some idea on not only what Tarot is and what it can be used for. My own fool's journey was laid down as a way for you to understand and reference the type of situations that could tie into anyone's journey.

During this project I have had to revisit many of my darkest moments and biggest traumas. It was not easy, and it highlighted some new areas for me to work on. I hope you have more of an appreciation for what the people behind the readings must try to deal with and balance every time they are requested to shuffle the path of the fool and lay it out for you.

Tarot readers, or anyone who works within the healing and guidance industry, be they Reiki Practitioners, Crystal Healers, Hypnotherapists or Therapists, all have a different motivation. Some are driven by a craving for fame, money, status, or other external factors. Like myself, many may not be driven by materialistic gains (I would do this all for free if

I didn't have bills to pay) and have come from a place of trauma, saw the benefits that holistic healing and readings have to offer and are driven by a real desire to make a difference. The way I look at it, if I have made someone's life better by doing what I'm doing I must be doing something right.

We are all different and just because you may have had one bad experience, please don't let it put you off trying it again with someone else. I'm sure there are plenty of clients who have come to me who might not have received what they expected, it just means that I'm not for them. I encourage everyone who comes to me to try someone else if they feel like that, because I want everyone to have the chance to experience the same positive changes that I did.

As with many who have suffered and flourished through a breakdown to finally reach a breakthrough, it can be a lonely place. But that doesn't mean it's not worth it, although I can't and won't speak for everyone on this. Since my journey began, I have found myself more solitary than before. I stand back in life and view it through these 78 cards and that's the connection I invest most of my energy in. Is it hard? Of course, it is, this book is testament to how difficult it has been for me. But it's the path I have chosen, and by joining me in this project I hope you agree with me that it was worth every disappointment.

Every time I complete a reading and walk away with the image of a client who has a little more faith in life than they did an hour before, every message I receive from someone who finally found the courage to take that step forward, and every referral to a friend because they have had great experience, make it worth it. For me this is not a job or career, it's a real passion. I'm not doing it to make a fortune for myself or line the pockets of others. I do it because I can see it makes a real difference. These pieces of colored card, these images filled with symbols and situations are not for everyone, but they can help anyone if the right steps are taken, and they are treated with respect.

Often, I am asked if anyone can read Tarot, the answer is always yes. Anyone can learn to do anything; I can draw a picture and most people can guess it's supposed to be a tractor. But I'm not an artist, nor do I kid myself that I could be. I can teach people to read cards in a day's workshop, but what makes a great card reader is someone who can be a great storyteller. Give me 3 cards and I can paint a life beyond anything you can dream. I can break your life down and expand in ways you cannot believe, if I wanted to, I could hit a nerve so hard that you would cry for days.

The difference between some card readers is how they view what they are doing. If they believe they are simply reading the cards, that's all they are doing. However, if you have been fortunate to find one who trusts the heart of the cards, who lets the cards come through how they want and acts as a conduit with no ulterior motives, you have found someone truly magnificent. Then my friend you are not only getting a card reading. You are getting a deep insight into your own world, its possibilities, obstacles, and advice. From there it is up to you what to do with it.

On the backside of that statement however, I do feel that there should be more expectations and accountability for people who read cards outside of a passive interest. I have developed myself extensively by completing specific training on not only reading cards, but also in therapy skills, communication training, some counselling workshops and behavioral therapy training. I believe that we have an important role in the development of those who bestow their trust on us. We are potentially clearing blockages and triggering traumatic memories and if we are not prepared to deal with that and expect to just walk away after a reading then we have failed in our duty.

Of course, my journey and opinions are unique to me and are, by no stretch of the imagination, final and applicable to everyone. Generally, the biggest thing with a Tarot reader is how they interpret the cards. If you have decided to seek guidance from a Tarot reader then you must trust them and at least be open to having your personal situation analyzed in a safe, professional environment where you can open and explore all aspects of your life without fear of judgement.

If that is not the experience you have, please don't let it put you off trying with one who has a better reputation or is known through a friend's referral.

Many wonderful people I have met on my journey, both as clients and practitioners, have taken something very hard in their life and used it to shape their future. If we let the mistakes of the past dictate our future and focus too much on our own regret, we will never be able to make that progress we need to experience the happy ending we all deserve. I truly hope that you can get something from this work to do the same.

We are all human (mostly at least) and we are all fighting a war of some kind. And if we lose sight of that then a lot of misunderstandings will occur. So please be kind to each other.

And finally, as I say at the end of every reading:

Thanks again for trusting me to share this experience with you. I wish you nothing but the best in every aspect of your life and may our paths cross if it's for our greater good. Don't be afraid to get in touch at any point. I'm always happy to help.

You take care my friends,

Andrew Greig

X

Printed in Great Britain
by Amazon

48383005R00145